WAYNE
GRETZKY

Hockey Player

Michael Benson

Ferguson

An imprint of ✓®Facts On File

Wayne Gretzky: Hockey Player

Ferguson
An imprint of Facts On File, Inc.
132 West 31st Street
New York NY 10001

Benson, Michael.
  Wayne Gretzky, hockey player/Michael Benson.
     p. cm.
  Includes index.
  Contents: Sent down from a higher league—The king of Wally's Coliseum—The majors—A unique combination—The Stanley Cup—California, here we come—Last days in the Big Apple—Time line—How to become an athlete—To learn more about athletes.
  ISBN 0-8160-5545-9 (alk. paper)
  1. Gretzky, Wayne, 1961—Juvenile literature. 2. Hockey players—Canada—Biography—Juvenile literature. [1. Gretzky, Wayne, 1961- 2. Hockey players.] I. Title.
  GV848.5.G73B48 2004
  796.962—dc22   2003023122

Ferguson books are available at special discounts when purchased in bulk quantities for businesses, associations, institutions, or sales promotions. Please call our Special Sales Department in New York at (212) 967-8800 or (800) 322-8755.

You can find Ferguson on the World Wide Web at http://www.fergpubco.com

Text design by David Strelecky

Pages 97–113 adapted from Ferguson's *Encyclopedia of Careers and Vocational Guidance, Twelfth Edition*

Printed in the United States of America

MP FOF 10 9 8 7 6 5 4 3 2 1

This book is printed on acid-free paper.

CONTENTS

1 Sent Down from a Higher League   1

2 The King of Wally's Coliseum   4

3 The Majors   16

4 "A Unique Combination"   32

5 The Stanley Cup   43

6 California, Here We Come   61

7 Last Days in the Big Apple   80

Time Line   94

How to Become a Professional Athlete   97

To Learn More about Professional Athletes   111

To Learn More about Wayne Gretzky and
  Hockey   114

Wayne Gretzky's Career Stats   117

Glossary   119

Index   121

1

SENT DOWN FROM A HIGHER LEAGUE

Wayne Gretzky holds so many National Hockey League (NHL) records that it would be easier to count the ones he does not have than the ones he does. All in all, according to the *NHL Official Guide and Record Book,* he holds 61 records. Forty of them are for things he accomplished in the regular season, 15 are for the Stanley Cup playoffs, and six were set in the NHL All-Star game.

Most notable among these records were most goals (894 of them, which broke Gordie Howe's record of 801) and most assists, which are counted when a player passes the puck to help set up a goal (1,963, way ahead of second-place Paul Coffey, who scored 1,102). He scored the most goals in the playoffs (122), including 24 game-winning goals, and had the most postseason assists (260). He scored the most goals in a season (92 in 1981–82) and the most assists in a season (163 in 1985–86). The record for most assists in a single game is seven. Wayne Gretzky is the only player to accomplish this feat, and he did it three times.

The Great Gretzky, as Wayne became known when he was still a teenager, stands head and shoulders above any hockey player who ever played. It almost seems as if he were sent down from a higher league to play in the NHL, but no higher league exists. Gretzky is just a natural talent. A lesser man might have allowed such superior playing skills to go to his head and become an unkind and egotistical person. But throughout his successful career, Wayne remained humble. He used his ever-growing celebrity to raise money for charity. He married the woman he loved and had five beautiful children. His behavior was always a tribute to his home country of Canada and to his chosen sport, ice hockey.

This is his story.

Wayne Gretzky holds the most records of any hockey player of all time. (Bruce Bennett Studios)

2

THE KING OF WALLY'S COLISEUM

Wayne Douglas Gretzky was born on January 26, 1961. He was the first child of Walter and Phyllis Gretzky, who lived in Brantford, Ontario, Canada. His father was a telephone repairman. Wayne later had three brothers—Keith, Glen, and Brent—and one sister, Kim.

At first there was nothing exceptional about the blond baby boy. As he grew to become a toddler, however, his exceptional coordination began to show. When he was a kid, Wayne was painfully shy and rarely spoke. The only time he ever came out of his shell was when he was playing sports. He especially enjoyed lacrosse and baseball. In fact, if you asked him even today, he would say that baseball is his favorite sport. But baseball definitely was not the sport at which he excelled. From the very first time he played ice hockey, Wayne exhibited an exceptional talent for the sport, and he only improved.

Hockey is the number-one sport in Canada. No other sport comes close in popularity. One reason for this is that, for much of the year in Canada, there is plenty of ice. Canadian winters are long and cold. The lakes and rivers freeze over solid.

In many parts of the United States, if a kid wants to learn to ice skate, he or she has to find a skating rink. But that is not true in Canada, where ice is easy to find and where kids learn to skate just about as soon as they can walk.

Wayne Gretzky learned how to ice skate on the Nith River when he was barely two years old. The river ran right behind his grandmother's house in the nearby town of Canning. His dad took home movies of Wayne's first time on skates. Today that film is shown at the Hockey Hall of Fame in Toronto.

Phyllis and Walter Gretzky would take Wayne to visit his grandmother, Mary Gretzky, on Saturdays. While Walter watched hockey on television, Wayne would play with his grandmother. He pretended to be a star hockey player, and she was the goalie. He would take off his shoes and slide on his socks across the polished floor as if he were skating.

Walter remembers: "He'd stride and pretend he was skating like the players on television. His grandmother bought him one of those little hockey sticks that you find in souvenir stands. And he'd have that stick and a little ball. His grandmother would sit in her big chair and she'd be his goaltender." Wayne's grandmother loved hockey as much as everyone else in the family. Her favorite player was Frank Mahovlich of the Toronto Maple Leafs.

In the United States, many kids have had the unfortunate experience of sending a baseball through a window. In Canada the same thing happens, but with hockey pucks. To a kid in Canada, the sound of shattering glass usually means that a "slap shot" has gone astray. Wayne's father recalls, "Wayne always had a hockey stick in his hands. I'll never forget the time Wayne's grandfather had just replaced a window in his house that Wayne had broken with a shot. My dad had just completed the task of putting a new window in and he was standing back, admiring his work when—smash!—Wayne took another shot at the side of the house and broke the window again. I can still see his grandfather chasing him with a hockey stick while his grandmother stood back and laughed her head off. His grandfather ended up putting a board in front of the window every time he figured we'd be coming over."

Wayne's love of sports came from his dad. According to Wayne's father: "I believe in sport. I believe that a kid who participates in sports ends up much more mature and much brighter than kids who don't. And they learn that if you want something, you have to work for it. I don't think I pushed any of my kids into sport. But I told them when they decided to go into a sport, I believed they shouldn't give it a half effort. Some people may say that's pushing, but I believe when you go into a sport, you have to try to do the best you can all the time. I don't believe in the philosophy that the kids should just be sent out to go have fun. To me, that's ridiculous. If the boy is sent out to do the best he can do, he's going to be happy."

Wayne loved hockey so much that going to the nearest pond or river to skate was too much work. Every winter he would shovel the snow off the backyard, mow the grass

Wayne (right) chats with his father, Walter, at a game.
(Bruce Bennett Studios)

very short, and then turn on the lawn sprinkler. When the water froze he would have a 60-foot by 40-foot skating rink in his own backyard.

Wayne's dad had built boards and put in goals, so the rink was called Wally's Coliseum, after Walter Gretzky. Wayne's friends and teammates would join him in Wally's Coliseum. There were even lights set up behind the Gretzky house so that hockey could be played at night.

"It was for self-preservation," Walter later said of the construction that had taken over his backyard. "I got sick of taking him to the park and sitting there for hours freezing to death."

First Goal

Wayne's first hockey team was the Nadrofsky Steelers, with whom he began playing when he was five. It was a local Brantford team that played in the Ontario Minor Hockey Association.

Although it might have been too early to know that Wayne was going to be the greatest hockey player of all time, people could tell from the start that he was special. When Wayne was five years old he was playing in the novice hockey league for nine- and 10-year-olds. He scored his first goal in that league at age five. The following year he scored 27 goals. He also earned his first trophy, the Wally Bauer Trophy, which was given to the most-improved player.

When he was seven years old he scored 104 goals. At eight he scored 196. Then, at age nine, when he was officially "old enough" to play in the league, he scored an unbelievable 378 goals. At one point in that season he scored 50 goals in six games.

It was at this time that Wayne first learned how to play against opponents who outweighed him by a large margin. This was a skill the rather lean Gretzky would later need when he played against the bruisers of the National Hockey League.

Playing for the Steelers, Wayne scored just about every time he handled the puck. He once entered a game in the third period with his team down 5-0 and quickly scored six goals to win the game 6-5.

It became clear to everyone that Wayne was in the wrong league. From then on, Wayne's coaches made every attempt to keep him on the ice with players who could provide him with proper competition. By the time he was 14, Wayne was playing with 20-year-olds.

As a kid, Wayne used a training technique that was more common in Russia than in Canada. While keeping a puck on his stick, he would skate around pylons set out on the ice. Skating around pylons was not common at the time, but years later, when it was learned that this was how Gretzky had practiced his skating and stickhandling, putting pylons on the ice became very popular.

At age 10, Wayne moved up in league and played with the major peewee division. He scored 104 goals at age 10, and 191 at age 11. By that time hockey fans were asking for his autograph, television crews were following him around, and reporters from big-time magazines such as *Sports Illustrated* were calling for interviews.

Gordie Howe, pictured here in 1962 after scoring his 500th goal, was Wayne's favorite hockey player growing up. (Associated Press)

Newspapers began to refer to Wayne as "the next Bobby Orr," one of the big hockey stars of the time. But Wayne had a different hockey superstar he wanted to be like, and as a kid he often told reporters so: "I don't want to be the next Bobby Orr," he said. "I want to be the next Gordie Howe."

In one of the first newspaper articles about Wayne, the 10-year-old fifth-grader said, "Gordie Howe is my kind of player. He had so many tricks around the net, no wonder he scored so many goals. I'd like to be just like him."

Dealing with Pressure

Years later, one of Wayne's former teammates from the Nadrofsky Steelers, Lenny Hachborn, said that even though Wayne was clearly a superior hockey player, back then Lenny would not have wanted to trade places with Wayne: "He had all that pressure. Everybody was always out for him, slashing him [hitting him with their sticks]. Even at that age. And there were all the problems with the parents who were jealous of how good he was. Most of the parents resented him. Now they are bragging that their kids once played with Wayne Gretzky."

There would be boos in the crowd when Wayne scored a goal. Worse, there would be cheers if he got knocked down.

Being a better hockey player than the other kids did not make Wayne happy. Most of the kids treated him nicely enough. But the parents of his teammates and the players on the other team often called him names like "hot dog" or "puck hog," which meant he was not allowing the other kids to play enough. Wayne knew that neither of those charges was fair. He shared the puck a lot and he never showed off. When he was 12 the criticism Wayne received became so great that he considered quitting. When he was 14 he began to play hockey in a different town. It was not because the competition was tougher, however. It was, as Wayne once explained, "because I had to get away from the people."

A National Story at 13

But Wayne didn't quit. He kept playing and kept getting better. By the time Wayne was 13, his dominance on the hockey rink was a well-known local story. When that season was over, he was a national story. His fame really began when his team traveled to Quebec City for a tournament. He put on such a dazzling display that the reporters from Montreal began to call him "Le Grand Gretzky," which translates as the Great Gretzky, a name that stuck and later became simply, the Great One.

The *Brantford Examiner* of April 10, 1974, announced: "Wayne Gretzky got the puck inside the Waterford blue line and let go with a slap shot. The Waterford goalie got a piece of the puck, but not enough to keep it from going in the net. Players rushed onto the ice and the game was held up for several minutes. Gretzky had scored his 1,000th career goal!"

During the 1973–74 season Wayne was chosen as a junior player to participate in a promotion at Toronto's Varsity Arena. He was allowed to take a penalty shot against goalie John Rea of the World Hockey Association's Toronto Toros. When it occurs in an actual game, a penalty shot is awarded to a player after he is illegally pulled down when he has the puck and is on a "breakaway," that is, with no one between him and the opposing goalie. For the penalty shot, the other players have to stand back while the shooter goes one-on-one against the goalie, skating in as close as he wants before he shoots the puck. Rea made the save (he kept the puck from going into the goal) and in a rare show of emotion, Wayne slammed his stick against the ice.

On November 27, 1976, Wayne played his first game in the Ontario Hockey Association, a league at the major junior A level. The Canadian newspaper the *Examiner*, said, "The Great Gretzky not only looked like he had been there for the entire season, he scored the game-winning assist." While playing for the Peterborough Petes of the Ontario Hockey League, Wayne scored three assists in three games.

The Great Greyhound

The following year Wayne was ready to join the minor league system, which funnels players upward toward the top: the National Hockey League. As is the case with most amateur players, Wayne would have to be "drafted" into the minor leagues by a professional team that was interested in him. But Wayne's father, Walter, decided that Wayne was too young to be away from home as much as he already was. Being drafted by a team in another part of Canada would only take him away for longer periods of time. Thus, Walter wrote to many teams outside the Brantford area, saying that Wayne would refuse to report to them if they took him in the draft.

Ultimately, Walter's ploy did not work. Wayne was drafted by the Sault (pronounced *soo*) Ste. Marie Greyhounds—a team to which Walter had not yet written. They talked things over with Walter, as well as with Wayne's new agent, Gus Badali, and arranged for Wayne to live in Sault Ste. Marie. They also agreed to put Wayne through college if he should get injured playing hockey.

In 1977–78 Wayne played a 64-game season with the Greyhounds. He scored 70 goals and 112 assists, the league-leader in both categories. He added another six goals and 20 assists in 13 postseason games.

As a Greyhound, Wayne wanted to wear number 9 on his sweater (which is what hockey players call their jerseys), the same number as his hero, Gordie Howe. But the number was already taken by a four-year veteran of the Greyhounds named Brian Gualazzi. So, unhappily, Wayne began the season with the uniform number 19. A few games into the season he switched to number 14. Midseason, the Greyhounds' general manager Murray "Muzz" MacPherson suggested that Wayne use number 99, which, he reasoned, was the next best thing to the number Wayne wanted. Wayne agreed, and he wore number 99 for the remainder of his career. In his first year as a Greyhound, Wayne won the league's Rookie of the Year award. He still qualified as a rookie because he had played only three games in the league the previous season.

At this time the NHL scouts were watching Wayne very carefully. They saw a future superstar and hoped he would skate in their league one day.

In December 1977 and January 1978 Wayne had his first opportunity to play in an international tournament. The World Junior Championships was specifically for players under 20 years old and was held in Quebec City, in Quebec, Canada. Playing in six games for the Canadian team—against the United States, the Soviet Union, Sweden, West Germany, and Czechoslovakia twice—Wayne scored eight goals and nine assists. Although Canada finished a disappointing third in the tournament, Wayne still distinguished himself by being named Best Forward.

3

THE MAJORS

The year 1972 marked a milestone in the history of hockey with the formation of a second major league: the World Hockey Association (WHA). The WHA was formed to compete against the monopoly that the NHL had over the sport. The WHA competed by doing away with some NHL restrictions. For example, the minimum age for an NHL player had always been 20, because the league did not want kids playing in the majors before they were ready—both emotionally and physically. The WHA had no such age limit, which meant good things for young talent like Wayne Gretzky. Thus, in 1978 Wayne signed his first big-league hockey contract with the Indianapolis Racers of the WHA.

Although Wayne was happy to finally be playing in the big leagues, the NHL was still considered the number-one hockey league. As long as Gretzky played in the WHA, the spotlight could never be completely on him.

Wayne's contract with the Racers referred to him as an underage junior. Just before Wayne's pro career began, there were some experts who were concerned. They saw him as a boy who was about to play against men. They feared that he was going to be overwhelmed, as much mentally as physically. "He's not going to be a star overnight," reporters predicted.

Wayne on the Indianapolis Racers, 1978 (Associated Press, Indianapolis Star/News)

Wayne ended up playing only eight games for the Racers. He scored three goals and three assists in that stretch. The Racers were short on cash, so Wayne and two other players were traded for cash and future draft picks.

Traded at 17

In November 1978 Wayne was traded to the Edmonton Oilers, another WHA team. Upon hearing of his trade, Wayne spoke to an Edmonton reporter about the pros and the cons of the move: "It's a big change, but I'm going to try to meet some kids there. Hopefully, I'm going to go to night school in January, so I'll get to know people there. And I'm pretty sure there's a girl I knew in Sault Ste. Marie who's moved out there."

Wayne had always been too busy being a hockey player to have a steady girlfriend. But not long after he joined the Oilers that changed. Her name was Vicky Moss. Wayne met her because her brother Joey worked in the Oilers' dressing room. Wayne and Vicky were together until 1987.

"Brinks"

In Edmonton Wayne established himself as a star at the top level. On November 3, 1978, Wayne played his first game with the Oilers. He wore jersey number 20. It was the last time in Wayne's pro career that he would wear a number other than the one he made famous. By the next game, his new Oiler jersey with the big 99 was ready for the Great One. Edmonton could quickly tell that their investment in Gretzky was going to be worthwhile. Attendance increased by 1,000 fans per game the instant he showed up.

Compared to the other Oilers, Gretzky was making a lot of money, and he was still a kid. His teammates began to call him "Brinks," after the famous armored trucks known for carrying money.

Getting Benched

On December 13, 1978, playing against Cincinnati, Edmonton Oilers coach Glen Sather benched Gretzky for not playing enough defense. The coach had told Wayne to stay back, but Wayne was spending more time trying to score and set up goals. The coach saw this as a key moment in Gretzky's career.

"He could have sulked, but Wayne got mad instead. Smoke was coming out of his ears. I think that game made Wayne Gretzky a hockey player. That night he stuck it to me."

After not playing for the first period, Gretzky was allowed to skate. He was not only more obedient when it came to following his coach's orders, but he also proved his own point. During times when it was appropriate for him to launch an attack, he scored three goals (which is called a

During his first season with the Edmonton Oilers, Wayne established himself as a top-level player. (Bruce Bennett Studios)

hat trick) in the last two periods of the game and led the Oilers to victory.

Dream Fulfilled

During the 1978–79 season Wayne was able to play in the WHA All-Star game, where he realized a dream. He skated on the same line as his hero Gordie Howe and Howe's son Marty. Gretzky scored the first goal from a Marty Howe pass, just 35 seconds into the first period. That year the WHA All Stars did not split into two squads and play against each other as they usually did. Instead they played against a team of Russian All Stars from Moscow, thus giving Wayne his second experience with international competition.

In 72 games that season, Wayne scored 43 goals and 61 assists, for a total of 104 points. In 13 playoff games, Wayne added another 20 points. He was named the WHA Rookie of the Year.

During the regular season the Oilers finished in first place, winning 48, losing 30, with two ties. In the play-offs—for the league's Avco Cup—they made it to the championship series but lost in the finals to Winnipeg.

Around this time the NHL began to look at the Gretzky situation with some concern. They wanted the greatest player in the world in their league, where he would boost attendance when playing on the road just as much as he did on his home ice. The league had assumed that sooner or later Wayne would switch to the NHL since many NHL teams could pay him more than a WHA team could. But the Oilers were paying Gretzky well, and they showed every sign of wanting to keep Gretzky for the foreseeable future. Those fears were realized when, on his 18th birthday, Gretzky skated out onto the center of the Edmonton ice and, before a roaring crowd, signed a 21-year contract.

The NHL still wanted Wayne, and they were persistent. If Gretzky were to remain an Oiler, the league decided, then the Oilers would have to leave the WHA and join the

Wayne on the night of his and the Oilers' last WHA game (Bruce Bennett Studios)

NHL. The NHL and the WHA came to a financial agreement. In the 1979–80 season the Oilers joined the NHL, and Wayne joined the big show.

"At least I scored a goal."

On October 10, 1979, Wayne scored his first NHL assist, setting up teammate Kevin Lowe in a game in Chicago. He scored his first goal four days later. The goalie who gave up that goal was Glen Hanlon of Vancouver. It happened in the third period of Wayne's third game. At the time he thought to himself: "If I never play in the NHL again, at least I scored a goal."

That season the Oilers added another teenager who would become a hockey legend to its roster. His name was Mark Messier, a hometown boy who had grown up in the suburbs of Edmonton.

On February 15, 1980, Wayne scored a record seven assists in one game. That set an NHL record tied only by

Gretzky himself (on December 11, 1985, and February 14, 1986). At 19 years and two months of age, he became the youngest NHL player ever to score 50 goals in a season.

That same year the NHL declared that Wayne could not win the NHL's Rookie of the Year award, which is called the Calder Trophy, because of his year in the WHA. However, he did win the Lady Byng Trophy, the NHL's sportsmanship award, in 1980. He also won the award in 1990–91, 1991–92, and 1993–94. But Gretzky lost out on the Most Valuable Player award, the Art Ross Trophy, to Marcel Dionne of the Los Angeles Kings.

During that season Wayne was again able to play with Gordie Howe, this time in the NHL All-Star game. That game was the first of 18 NHL All-Star games in which Wayne would play: 1980–86, 1988–94, and 1996–99.

Gretzky's first NHL postseason was a short one. The Oilers lost three straight games in the first round to the Philadelphia Flyers. Still, the exposure of that first NHL season made Gretzky a household name. When asked to name one hockey player, even people who did not follow hockey at all now said "Wayne Gretzky."

Patience and Anticipation

Of Wayne's hockey skills, his father Walter says, "Patience is one of his most underrated assets. He's like a vulture, the way he waits for somebody to make a mistake. When the other team doesn't make many mistakes, Wayne isn't that noticeable."

Another key word in Wayne's game was "anticipation." About Wayne's play with the great Edmonton Oilers teams, Gretzky biographer Andrew Podnieks wrote, "Gretzky and the Oilers never reacted to a game—they anticipated play. They knew what would happen next not as it was happening, but *before* it happened. Gretzky always broke out of his own zone really early, while the other team still had the puck. . . . He knew that his man would be looking for a fast break, and he knew that the pass would get to open ice if he were there for it."

The NHL was an old-fashioned league, in which many teams played a slower and less-exciting style that had been popular since the league was born in 1917. But the Oilers did not play in an old-fashioned way. They were like a fast-break team in basketball. Their game was stealing the puck and then moving toward the other team's goal as fast as possible.

Like basketball's Larry Bird, Wayne knew where he was at all times during a game, and he knew where everything else was, too. He played as if he had extra sets of eyes on the sides and back of his head. It seemed as if he could see the entire skating surface at once.

Wayne changed the way hockey was played with his behavior behind his opponent's goal. He would camp out back there and make the defense come to him. Because of his speed they had to come at him two at a time. Gretzky would then score assist after assist with centering passes to his newly unguarded teammates.

Gretzky not only passed the puck better than anyone ever had, but he had a great shot on goal as well. He could hit the smallest opening with accuracy. Because he was so skinny, goalies were often unpleasantly surprised by how hard Wayne's shot was. Goalies called his shots "sneaky fast."

Wayne also had a way of never hitting the puck with the same rhythm twice that made his shots harder to time, and therefore more difficult for the goalie to block.

Player of the Year—Every Year

Gretzky did not have to play in the NHL long before he started breaking records. When he entered the league, the record for most points (goals and assists added together) in a season was held by Phil Esposito, who had 152 (divided evenly: 76 goals and 76 assists). In his second season in the league, Gretzky blew that record away, scoring 164 points. Up until that time Bobby Orr held the record for most assists in a season, with 102. But that record fell that season as well, as Wayne had 109 assists. Esposito's record of 76 goals in a season was the only single-season scoring record left standing, but it was teetering and would only last one more year.

In 1981 *The Sporting News* named Wayne the NHL Player of the Year. He won the award for seven straight seasons: 1980–81 through 1986–87. In 1981 Gretzky also won the first of 10 Art Ross memorial trophies, awarded to the NHL's leading scorer (1980–81 through 1986–87, 1989–90, 1990–91, and 1993–94).

The Oilers made it into the postseason in 1981 despite the fact that their record was only 14th best in the league. (The top 16 teams play in the NHL postseason.) In the first round the Oilers were slated to meet the Montreal Canadiens, one of the most powerful teams in the league. They had finished on top in their division, the Norris Division, and had the third-best record in the league.

The Oilers were psyched for the best-of-five series, and Wayne received extra incentive to play hard when the Canadiens' top star, Guy Lafleur, told a reporter that he planned to put Gretzky in his "back pocket." Gretzky and the Oilers came out hot for the first game of the series in Montreal and won 6-3. Gretzky was credited with an assist on five of the six Oiler goals. After the final Oiler score, Gretzky skated slowly past the Canadiens' bench and touched his back pocket.

The Oilers kept the momentum by defeating Montreal in Game 2 by a score of 3-1, also on the Canadiens' home ice. That meant that the series moved to Edmonton, with the Oilers needing only one more win to boot the

Canadiens out of the playoffs. The Oilers did just that, defeating the Canadiens 6-2 in Game 3 to sweep the series and send the Montreal players home for the summer.

Next up for the Oilers were the defending Stanley Cup champions, the New York Islanders, who played in the Nassau County Coliseum on Long Island. The Islanders were the best team in the league and, against the Oilers, they skated like it. They won the best-of-seven series in six games, and it was the Oilers' turn to go home. The Oilers had lost, but it had not been for lack of trying. The team, including Gretzky, held nothing back. But the Islanders were too strong.

Gretzky and the Oilers played nine postseason games in 1981. Wayne scored 21 points.

Canada Cup

That same year Wayne once again had an opportunity to skate for his country. Naturally, he thought that playing for Team Canada in the Canada Cup tournament was going to be one of the highlights of his life. To say that he was disappointed with the reality of the tournament would be an understatement. He later said that it was the "worst experience" he had in his hockey career.

The tournament itself began a year late. It was originally scheduled for 1980, but a boycott of that year's Summer Olympics in Moscow made it impossible to hold

The 1981 Canada Cup tournament was, for Wayne, one of the biggest letdowns of his career. (Bruce Bennett Studios)

a hockey tournament that year. Plans to hold the tournament in 1981 ran late, so Team Canada had to train hard and quickly to get into shape.

For Team Canada the tournament started out solidly enough. In the first game of the round-robin part of the tournament they defeated Finland 9-0. The second game went equally well, as the Canadians beat the United States 8-3 with Gretzky scoring twice and adding two assists. Things went downhill from there.

The Canadians could manage only a 4-4 tie in their third game. Gretzky's line—which also featured Guy Lafleur and Gil Perreault—was held scoreless. Although Canada won their next game 4-3 over Sweden, Gretzky was struck in the elbow by an opponent's stick (which is called being slashed), and Perreault broke his ankle. Perreault was off of skates for weeks. Gretzky kept playing in the tournament with his injured elbow, but the quality of his play suffered. Gretzky said that, up until that time, it was the most severe injury he had ever suffered. Perreault was replaced on Gretzky's line by Marcel Dionne. The next game was against the young but powerful Soviet Union team, and Canada won 7-3. Canada beat the U.S. for a second time, 4-1, to complete the round-robin.

The two teams with the best records in the tournament then played for the world championship. Those teams were Canada and the Soviet Union. Of course, that was the matchup that Canadians had wanted. But the Canadian team may have gone into the finals somewhat overconfident because they had handled the Soviets easily earlier in the tournament. The Soviets eventually beat up on the Canadians, winning the game and the Canada Cup with an 8-1 victory. Although Wayne had led the tournament in scoring, he was hurting and he felt that he had let his country down.

Change of Style

Wayne spent five days in Florida after the tournament nursing his wounds and thinking about his future. He decided that his playing style had become too predictable. Opposing defensemen knew that he preferred to pass the puck rather than shoot on goal. He had developed a reputation and his opponents were starting to make the correct play against him. He decided that in the upcoming season he would change up his previous pattern. He was going to pass the puck less and shoot on goal more.

He carried out his plan, and the results showed in his statistics. He had the single greatest season by one player in the history of hockey.

In the 1981–82 season Gretzky was on the ice for more minutes than any other player in the league. He always skated on a power play when his team had one extra player because the other team had a man in the penalty box. He also skated when the Oilers had a man in the penalty box. He scored 92 goals during that season, 37 more than the previous season. Six of those goals came when his team was shorthanded—that is, they were killing a penalty, or getting through the two minutes without having a goal scored against them. While other teams dawdled and played defense while waiting out penalties, the Oilers saw being a man down as another opportunity to score. Wayne scored 10 hat tricks that season—another record.

What Gretzky had not counted on was that his assists would increase in the 1981–82 season as well. Since he had varied his style and defensemen in the league could not be sure if he was going to pass or not, Gretzky's passes were that much more effective. After scoring 109 assists during 1980–81, he upped that number to 120 assists the following season. Gretzky's decision to plague the goalies of the NHL with his slap shots not only turned him into a better hockey player—something that most fans did not even think was possible—but it made all of his teammates better, as well. The Edmonton Oilers were playing a brand of hockey that no one had seen before or could even have imagined.

Until Gretzky entered the league, scoring 100 points in a season was a sign of excellence, much like knocking in 100 runs during a season is a standard of excellence in baseball. In the 1981–82 season Gretzky scored his 100th point during the 38th game of the season. He still had more than half a season to go.

4

"A UNIQUE COMBINATION"

During the 1981–82 season the Oilers' coach Glen Sather commented on Gretzky's greatness. He said, "There is no one area that makes him superior. It's a unique combination of all areas. Technically, he is the best player I have ever seen. Watch him move the puck from side to side on his stick, watch him pass to the left, to the right. His hand-eye coordination is extraordinary. His reflexes are uncanny. Where he is unmatched is in the reflexes, the split-second acrobatics, in doing instantly what his brain says has got to be done."

At any given moment during a game, Wayne knew in which direction the skaters were heading and how fast. He seemed to know this information instinctively, since he did not have to see it to know it. He knew what was happening behind his back just as well as he knew what was happening in front of him.

The Oilers finished that season with 48 wins, 17 losses, and 15 ties. They scored 417 goals, or 5.21 goals per game. That year the Oilers, who were favored to become the next Stanley Cup champions, played the Los Angeles Kings in the first round of the playoffs.

The postseason got off to a miserable start for the Oilers. In the first game against the Kings, they built up an early 4-1 lead. The game turned into one in which both teams were playing offense and no one was playing defense. The Oilers lost their lead and ended up losing the game by a somewhat ridiculous score of 10-8. Things improved in

Celebrating a job well done (Bruce Bennett Studios)

Game 2. With the score tied 2-2 after three periods of play, Wayne scored in overtime to bring the Oilers to victory, and to tie the series at one game apiece.

The Oilers' problems with losing their lead reemerged in Game 3. They were ahead 5-0 in the final period and then completely fell apart. They allowed the Kings to score five times in the third period, sending the game into overtime. The Kings then scored the winning goal and took a two-to-one lead in the series.

That match did not win Gretzky any new fans for a couple of reasons. While Edmonton was in the process of blowing its lead, a fight broke out and everyone on the ice went at it—except Wayne. Five Kings fought against four Oilers while Wayne alone followed the referee's instructions to leave the first two fighters alone. The other nine players received 10-minute misconduct penalties while Wayne was allowed to continue in the game. After the game one of the Kings players told a reporter, "Gretzky is just a player who likes to score goals, but I consider him one of the worst team players in the league."

The Oilers tied the series again with a 3-2 victory in Game 4, sending the series to Edmonton for the final game. Despite skating on their home ice, the Oilers lost Game 5 by a score of 7-4 and were eliminated from the playoffs.

In the spring of 1982 Wayne once again had an opportunity to play for Team Canada, this time in the World

Hockey Championships held in Finland. Since the tournament was held at the same time as the Stanley Cup playoffs, Wayne would not have been able to play had the Oilers not been eliminated in the first round. The opportunity to play in the World Championships did not completely soothe the pain of his team's loss to the Kings, but it helped. Wayne saw the tournament in Finland as a chance to make up for the bad showing he felt he made in the 1981 Canada Cup tournament.

While Wayne was playing in the World Championships in Europe, Peter Pocklington, the owner of the Oilers, was held hostage in his own home by a madman who had broken in and demanded $1 million. The police eventually arrested the kidnapper after a shoot-out in which a bullet grazed Pocklington's arm. It was hard for Wayne to concentrate on hockey in Europe when such strange and scary things were going on back at home. However, he gave it his best and proved to be the best player in the tournament, even though Team Canada only came in third, winning a bronze medal.

Other Pursuits

During the off-season between 1981–82 and 1982–83, Wayne went to the Soviet Union to hold a clinic. In Europe he was known as the "King of Hockey." In the Soviet Union a film crew followed him, making a documentary about the talented player.

Back in Canada Wayne did more charity work. He raised money for the Canadian National Institute for the Blind by holding a celebrity tennis tournament. He also entered the business end of hockey for the first time when he purchased just less than half of the Belleville Bulls, a minor league team.

Wayne also spent many days during that off-season making TV commercials. He endorsed everything from 7UP soda to Bic pens and razors.

Changing the Flow

Gretzky's hockey skills were so much better than everyone else's that he changed the flow of every game in which he played. Before he arrived on the scene, the flow of play always involved passing the puck to the head skater while charging toward the other team's goal. This was the best way to avoid being offside (a type of violation), since no attacking player, according to the rules, was allowed to cross the blue line before the puck.

The former Boston Bruins general manager Harry Sinden once explained how this changed when Gretzky was on the ice: "He was the first one to make the late man coming into the zone . . . the most dangerous man. Gretzky could hold onto the puck for so long, turning toward the boards and stickhandling in place, that even if you knew what he was going to do you couldn't stop him."

Gretzky would eventually pass the puck, with pinpoint accuracy, to a teammate who had skated in front of the other team's goal. The teammate, who was sometimes behind Gretzky and seemingly out of his field of vision, would score and Gretzky would have another assist.

Like Trying to Catch Confetti

The National Hockey League is a violent place, where injuries are frequent, fights break out in nearly every game, and some players are valued for their meanness even more than for their hockey talent.

Given that, many wondered how the mild-mannered Gretzky survived, even dominated, and remained unharmed. There were a couple of reasons for this. For starters, Wayne did not like to fight. Because of his slender size and peace-loving style, he avoided confrontation whenever he could. Another reason was that he skated so well that he was very difficult to hit. Coach Sather said that trying to hit Gretzky was like trying to "catch confetti." New York Islander Bill Torrey said that Gretzky was like "an eel who's hard to hit because he's not around the boards much."

During the 1982–83 season the Oilers continued to play their highly entertaining lots-of-offense, not-much-defense brand of hockey. They averaged more than five goals per game. In almost half of the games they played that year,

Hockey can be violent at times, and Wayne avoided fighting. Unfortunately, he took his share of attacks from other players. (Bruce Bennett Studios)

the total number of goals scored by both teams was greater than 10. While the Edmonton fans knew they had the greatest show on ice right there in their hometown, around the rest of the hockey world there was not universal praise for the Oilers' way of playing. Hockey fans were used to games being won or lost by scores such as 3-1 or 4-2. Edmonton's games weren't like that. They won 11-8 and 9-7.

There was only one way for the Oilers to silence their critics—and that was to win the Stanley Cup. Until they proved they were the best team in the NHL, they were going to have to put up with the writers and fans who did not like their style.

A Star on and off the Ice

Gretzky's totals at the end of the 1982–83 season were once again mind-boggling, but down slightly from the previous season. He scored 71 goals and 125 assists, for a total of 196 points. He won the scoring title by 72 points. In fact, he had more assists than the second-place scorer (Peter Stastny, of the Quebec Nordiques) had total points.

One of the reasons Wayne's scoring numbers were down was that he played less. Coach Sather hoped that by giving Wayne more of a rest during each game, this valuable player would have more energy left in his tank at the end of the season for the all-important playoffs. Wayne played an average of 26 minutes per game during the 1981–82 season. In 1982–83 that time was down to 22 minutes.

About Gretzky's reduced playing time Sather said, "Wayne played far too much last year. . . . We want to come a lot closer to winning the Cup than we did last spring."

Indeed, Wayne's fame meant that he had to face much more during a season than any other hockey player did. Every time the Oilers visited another city, the local television talk shows would want Wayne to be a guest. Reporters asked him 20 questions for every one they asked a teammate. Fans swarmed him for autographs. And Wayne had trouble saying no to anyone.

But none of this could slow him down. In 1983 Wayne set an All-Star game record by scoring four goals in one period.

Captain Gretzky

During the 1982–83 season Wayne was named captain of the Oilers. That meant that he was the team's leader on the ice. The captain of a hockey team gets to wear a "C" on the shoulder of his sweater. From that point on Wayne was the captain of whichever team he played for, throughout the remainder of his career.

When it came to keeping Wayne from becoming exhausted for the playoffs, Sather's plan worked. The Oilers not only finished first in their division, Wayne hit the ice for the playoffs feeling fresh and ready. Edmonton played the Winnipeg Jets in the opening round. In the first game, played in Edmonton, Wayne was on fire. Before his home crowd, he scored four goals and added an assist. Although he only managed three assists in the remaining two games, Edmonton defeated the Jets three straight to move into the next round.

That brought on the Calgary Flames in the second round. In that best-of-seven series, Edmonton defeated the Flames four games to one. In Game 3, Wayne scored an incredible seven points, with four goals and three assists. Wayne scored 14 points against Calgary, despite being held pointless in Game 1. The Oilers were on a roll.

Next up in the Stanley Cup semifinals were the Chicago Blackhawks. Once again Wayne got the series off to a strong start, scoring one goal and adding four assists in Game 1 played in Chicago. The Oilers went on to sweep the Blackhawks in four straight games, with Wayne scoring a total of two goals and 10 assists.

That put the Oilers in the finals. Their opponents were the New York Islanders, the defending Stanley Cup champions. Against the Islanders, who appeared to be the better team right from the start, the Oilers were no longer able to control the tempo of the game.

There would be no 12-9 scoring games in this series. In fact, in Game 1, the Oilers were not able to score at all. New York won the opener in Edmonton by a score of 2-0, which was by now a very un-Oilers-like score. In Game 2 things turned ugly when the Islanders goalie, Billy Smith, sent Gretzky sprawling to the ice when he hit him with his stick. Smith was sent to the penalty box for five minutes and Gretzky went on to have his worst playoff series ever, scoring no goals and only four assists. The Islanders won four straight and kept the Stanley Cup. The Oilers had to wait for their next chance at the Cup.

When it was over Gretzky admitted that the Islanders had won not because they had greater hockey skills, but because they were tougher. "They took more punishment than we did," Wayne said. "They dove into more boards, stuck their faces in front of more pucks, threw their bodies into more pileups. They sacrificed everything they had."

During that off-season Wayne dabbled in show business. He tried being a singer, performing Charlie Daniels's "The Devil Went Down to Georgia" on *The Alan Thicke Show*. He tried a little acting, playing a villain on the daytime drama

Gretzky wrangles for the puck with the New York Islanders.
(Bruce Bennett Studios)

The Young and the Restless. Some said he wasn't bad; others said he shouldn't quit his day job.

Still, Wayne's fame expanded beyond the world of hockey. The Mattel toy company made a Gretzky action figure. American pop artist Andy Warhol painted a picture of Gretzky, and Wayne then posed for photographers with the artist and the painting. Gretzky had officially become a celebrity figure and was known by millions of people across the world.

5

THE STANLEY CUP

Until the 1983–84 season the record for at least one point scored in consecutive games was 30, and it was held by Gretzky. But that year Gretzky smashed the record—again. Beginning with the opening game of the season, Gretzky scored a point in 51 straight games. The streak came close to ending several times. The closest call came in the 44th game, when Wayne scored a goal with two seconds left in the third period—into an empty net. It is a common strategy, at the end of a hockey game, for the team that is behind to take their goalie off the ice and replace him with an offensive player. The extra skater sometimes helps the losing team catch up, but the strategy can also backfire. The empty goal makes for an inviting target and often leads to the winning team expanding its lead. In this case, that was exactly what happened.

Wayne's biggest night of the streak came against the New Jersey Devils, in game 21. The Oilers won 13-4, and Gretzky scored or assisted in eight of his team's goals.

The streak might have been considerably longer if it had not been for some bad luck. In the 52d game, versus Los Angeles, Gretzky fed teammate Charlie Huddy a precision pass while the opposing goalie was out of position. But Huddy's shot was wide and he missed the goal.

Soon after the streak ended Gretzky suffered a shoulder injury and missed six games. It had been four years since Gretzky had missed a game.

That season the Oilers had a record four players who scored more than 100 points. They were Gretzky, Paul Coffey, Jari Kurri, and Mark Messier. A fifth player almost joined their ranks, as Glenn Anderson finished the campaign with 99 points. Gretzky led the scoring, of course. He had 205 points during the season, the second of four times he would break the 200-point mark.

Finally, the Cup

The Oilers finished the season with the best win-loss record in the NHL. They won 57 games, lost 18, and played five ties. But the regular season mattered little. They had gotten themselves into the playoffs and would not be happy until they won the most-coveted prize in hockey, the Stanley Cup.

They played the Winnipeg Jets in the first round and had no trouble with them, sweeping their way into the second round with three consecutive victories. Things became more difficult for the Oilers in the second round when they played the Calgary Flames. The series went the full seven games, but the Oilers emerged victorious with a 7-3 win in the final contest.

That put Edmonton into the Stanley Cup finals, where their opponent was the defending champion New York Islanders. The Oilers were a high-scoring team, but they could manage only one goal against the Islanders in the first game of the series. Luckily for them, that was enough to win the game, played on the Islanders' home ice, 1-0. It was the lowest scoring contest of the year for the team. The Oilers were defeated 6-1 on Long Island the next night. Tied at one game apiece, the series moved to Edmonton. On their home ice, the Oilers won three straight—by scores of 7-2, 7-2, and 5-2—to win the Stanley Cup.

Wayne's parents and little brother Brent were in the stands for the final game. During the postgame celebration, while other Oilers skated around the ice holding up the Stanley Cup, Wayne picked up his brother—who was still small enough to be picked up—and skated around the ice with him. Even today, when asked, Wayne will say that winning the Stanley Cup for the first time was the biggest thrill of his hockey career. The days of journalists and fans poking fun at the Oilers' free-skating style were officially over.

Not Just a Symbol

The Stanley Cup is not just a symbol. It is an actual trophy and there is only one—the same one that was built for Lord Stanley back in the 19th century. The team that wins the Cup gets to keep it for a year. If another team wins the Cup the following year, they get it. Teams usually allow each player on the team to keep the Cup for a period of time before passing it along.

The day after Gretzky's greatest victory, he and a few of his teammates took the Cup from place to place in Edmonton so that their fans would get a chance to touch it.

Winning the Canada Cup

During that off-season Wayne had minor surgery on his ankle to remove bone chips. By August 1984 he had recovered and was ready to play for Team Canada in the Canada

Beaming with pride after the Oilers won the 1984 Stanley Cup (Bruce Bennett Studios)

Cup. This was the fourth time that Gretzky had played for his country, and the first three had not gone well. Before the 1984 tournament, it was thought that Canada's toughest competition would come from the Soviet Union. That turned out to be true, as Canada's only loss in the tournament came to the Soviets in an early round-robin. But when it came to the finals, the Soviets were gone and Canada played Sweden, who they defeated to win the Canada Cup.

1,000 Points

Before Gretzky came along, the player to most quickly score 1,000 points in the NHL was Hall of Famer Guy Lafleur, who had scored his thousandth point in his 720th game. On December 19, 1984, Gretzky shattered that record by scoring his thousandth point in his 424th game. Gretzky was only in his fifth season. He was 23 years old.

Wayne broke the record during a six-point scoring barrage against the Los Angeles Kings. His accomplishments were so astounding, so out-of-this-world, that fans stopped being astonished by him. He could no longer be judged on the same scale as the other players in the league.

Gretzky again scored more than 200 points during the 1984–85 season, the third time in his career he had done so, with 73 goals and 135 assists. In second place for the NHL scoring title that season was Peter Stastny, who had 135 total points, 73 points behind Gretzky. The Oilers won

49 games during the season and in 27 of them they scored seven or more goals.

Sometime during that season the welcome sign in Wayne's hometown of Brantford, Ontario, was altered forever. The sign now read, "Welcome to Brantford, home of Wayne Gretzky."

A Day in the Life

That season Wayne told a magazine interviewer what a day in the life of Wayne Gretzky was like: "The night before a game, I'm always in bed before 10:30. I'm up around 8:30 in the morning, have a cup of tea and something light to eat, like a piece of toast, and read the newspaper. I'll go to the rink where we'll practice at 10:30 and after practice, about 12:30, I eat. Then I spend the rest of the afternoon watching the soap operas. I go down to the rink at about 4 or 5. When I get to the rink, I'll play Ping-Pong with a couple of the guys. Most of the guys show up about 5:30 except for about six of us. Ping-Pong loosens me up and takes my mind off what's going to happen."

Gretzky, who is superstitious like many athletes, told the interviewer that he always put his uniform on in the same order. He always missed his first practice shot during warm-ups wide to the right, and just before the game he would drink a Diet Coke, ice water, Gatorade, and then another Diet Coke.

After being a hockey player for so long, Wayne had developed other likes, dislikes, and routines. For example, Wayne started playing hockey using a wooden stick but switched to an aluminum stick halfway through his professional career. He liked his stick blade to be stiff. The switch to aluminum came when he found that the metal stick was just as stiff as a wooden one but weighed much less. He could generate more stick speed with the aluminum stick, and therefore shoot and pass the puck faster. Despite the changes in sticks over the years, one thing never changed: the way that Wayne taped up his stick.

At a press conference Wayne once explained his taping style: "I use black tape that has white baby powder

Over the years Wayne developed strict habits and training routines to perfect his play. (Bruce Bennett Studios)

sprinkled on it. I find that when the puck is spinning, the black tape seems to catch it and stop it from spinning. As far as the baby powder goes, I use it because the stick will collect snow along the bottom and the baby powder stops it from sticking."

Defending the Cup

The Oilers cruised into the 1985 playoffs. Again, a successful regular season meant nothing. They were the defending Stanley Cup champions and would not be happy until they won the Cup for another year. For a time it looked like they were going to get to keep the Cup without losing a single postseason game. They defeated the Los Angeles Kings in three consecutive games and then moved past the Jets with four consecutive victories. Not all of the games were easy victories, but there were no defeats.

Things became more difficult in the semifinals when they needed six games to get past the Chicago Blackhawks. That put them into the finals against the Philadelphia Flyers. The Flyers managed only one win in the series. The Oilers won the series in five games, keeping the Stanley Cup for another year. Gretzky was the postseason's MVP, scoring 17 goals and 30 assists in his team's 18 playoff games.

Once again, Wayne received abundant praise for this unique playing style. In the September 29, 1985, edition of the *New York Times Magazine*, Mordecai Richler wrote:

"Gretzky strikes me as the first nondescript hockey star. Sometimes you don't even realize that he's out there, watching as he whirls, until he emerges out of nowhere, finding open ice, and accelerating to score. Other times, working out of a seemingly impossible angle in the corner, he can lay such a gift of a feathery pass right on the stick of whoever has skated into the slot."

A Season of Ups and Downs

During the 1985–86 season Gretzky, breaking his own record, had the greatest single season in league history. He set the NHL single-season scoring record with 215 points (52 goals, 163 assists). Second place in that season's scoring race went to Mario Lemieux, then in his second year in the league, who had 141 total points, 74 less than Gretzky. The hulking Lemieux was widely considered the second-best player in the league.

The 1985–86 Edmonton Oilers were one of the greatest teams in hockey history. Out of 80 games, they lost only 17 times. They scored 426 goals. That is 5.3 goals per game. Gretzky, who played in all 80 games, was held pointless only three times.

Perhaps the Oilers thought that, considering the ease with which they cruised to victory after victory during the regular season, winning the playoffs and the Stanley Cup for a third straight time would be just as easy. As it turned out, they could not have been more wrong.

The postseason started out well enough, with a three-game sweep of the Vancouver Canucks. In the second round the Oilers faced the Calgary Flames, a rival because both Edmonton and Calgary were in the Canadian province of Alberta.

The teams split the series' first six games. The seventh and final game would decide who continued on in the playoffs. In that final game the score was tied 2-2 when Edmonton defenseman Steve Smith attempted a cross-ice pass in his own end and accidentally banked the puck off Oiler goalie Grant Fuhr into his own net to score a goal for the other team. Edmonton's season was over.

After the loss 25-year-old Gretzky, clearly upset, said about himself, "I don't see Wayne Gretzky playing much longer."

The off-season, already destined to be a long and sad one, was complicated with stories in the media saying that some Oilers were spending too much time partying and not enough time sleeping on nights before hockey games. No players were named and nothing ever came of the accusations. But Gretzky and his teammates, still in mourning over a lost season, had to answer questions about their behavior both on and off the ice.

Hunger Pangs—and a Third Cup

The disappointment of the previous season made the Oilers hungry for victory heading into the 1986–87 season.

Although their statistics were not as sensational as the previous year, they still had the best record in hockey, with 50 victories. They outscored all other teams by more than 50 goals. Gretzky passed a couple more milestones, scoring his 500th goal and his 1,500th point.

There was no All-Star game that year. Instead, the NHL All-Star team played a two-game series against a Russian All-Star team. The event was called Rendezvous '87. Each country won a game, but Gretzky was clearly the best player on the ice in both matches. The two teams would meet again, memorably, in that year's Canada Cup tournament.

The Oilers' hunger panged harder as the playoffs began. They were determined not to go home early as they had the previous year. The format was changed a bit from previous years. Traditionally the first round of the playoffs had been best-of-five series that could be won with three victories. Now the first round would be the same as the other rounds and consist of a best-of-seven series, which required four wins.

In the opening round the Oilers faced the Los Angeles Kings and beat them in five games. The score of one of those games was 13-3 in the Oilers' favor, with 13 goals setting the record for most scored by a team in a single playoff game. Gretzky was involved in seven of the 13, with one goal and six assists.

The Oilers met the Winnipeg Jets in the second round and defeated them in four straight. Wayne scored one goal

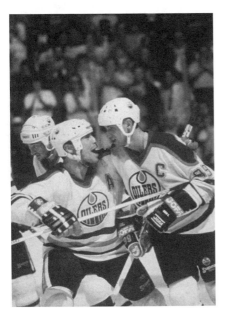

Mark Messier and Wayne Gretzky (Bruce Bennett Studios)

and five assists against the Jets. In the final game, with Oilers' victory assured, the Jets' Dale Hawerchuck gave Gretzky a cheap shot. The Great One hit the ice hard and suffered a mild concussion. However, because the Oilers had made such quick work of the Jets, Gretzky had nine days to recover before the semifinal series began against the Detroit Red Wings.

It took the Oilers five games to get past the Red Wings. The Red Wings won Game 1, and then lost four in a row. Perhaps still feeling the effects of his concussion, Wayne was held scoreless by the Red Wings and managed only two assists in the series.

In the finals the Oilers played the Philadelphia Flyers. The final series went to a seventh and final game. With the score tied one apiece in the second period, Gretzky made one of his trademark perfect passes to Jari Kurri who scored to put the Oilers on top for good. With 11 points in the series, Gretzky was clearly back to normal. The Oilers scored another goal in the third period but the Flyers were done, and Edmonton once again possessed the Stanley Cup.

Even though the season had a happy ending for Gretzky, he once again hinted that retirement was on his mind, just as he had the previous season.

"For me, personally, this has been the toughest year I've ever had," Gretzky said after the final game against the Flyers. "I don't know what my future holds for me right now. I'm probably more drained now than I've ever been. . . . People say there is an unwritten rule that you can't hit Gretzky—but that is not true."

But two months later, when training camp started for the Canada Cup tournament, Gretzky was on the ice for Canada's team with number 99 on his back.

Janet Jones

In 1987 Wayne broke up with his longtime girlfriend, Vicky Moss. Soon thereafter, he began to date a beautiful blond woman named Janet Jones, who was originally from St. Louis, Missouri.

When Wayne met Janet she lived in Los Angeles where she had worked as a model and actress, appearing in the movies *The Flamingo Kid*, *American Anthem*, *A Chorus Line*, and *Police Academy 5*. In the press, the pair quickly earned comparisons to the British royal couple Prince

Charles and Princess Diana, who were very popular media figures at the time.

The 1987 Canada Cup

In what has been called one of the great moments in hockey history, Gretzky set up the play that won the Canada Cup in 1987. In the finals of the Canada Cup tournament, Team Canada played the Soviet Union in a best-of-three series.

The first two games both went to double overtime. The Soviets took the opener and Canada won the second game, each by identical 6-5 scores. In the second game Gretzky was on the ice almost all the time and scored five assists. But Gretzky's stunning play came in the deciding Game 3. Late in the third period with the score tied at five goals apiece, Gretzky led a rush across the Soviet blue line, only to drop a no-look pass onto the stick of Mario Lemieux, who blasted home what turned out to be the winning goal. Of the 11 goals scored by Lemieux during the series against the Soviets, nine had come following passes by Gretzky.

The most enduring image of the Cup competition came seconds after Lemieux scored the winning goal. He leaped over a Soviet defenseman's stick and jumped into the arms of an elated Wayne Gretzky. Hockey's two greatest players embraced in celebration.

Injuries and Victory

For the first time in his career, Gretzky did not lead the league in combined goals and assists during the 1987–88 season. He had 149 points, which was second in the league to Mario Lemieux's 168. Wayne had a good excuse for the second-place finish. He missed 13 games midseason because of a sprained knee. He was back in action in time for that season's NHL All-Star game, but the star of that show was Lemieux. A week after the All-Star game Gretzky was injured again, this time when he was struck in the eye by a hockey stick early in a game between Edmonton and Pittsburgh. He suffered a slight scratch of his cornea and missed three more games. Most players who return from such injuries choose to wear a protective eye visor afterward, but Gretzky did not. He told reporters that he had tried wearing a visor in the past but had taken it off.

In February Wayne announced that he was engaged to Janet Jones and that they were to be married that July. On March 1, 1988, Wayne passed Gordie Howe to become NHL all-time assist leader with assist number 1,050 against Los Angeles.

The Oilers won 44 games during the season and Gretzky was fully recovered from his injury by the time the playoffs began. The team had had stronger regular seasons in the past, but when it came to the postseason, they were an unstoppable force.

The Oilers faced the Jets in the opening round and defeated them four games to one. Gretzky scored one goal and 10 assists versus the Jets. That brought on the Calgary Flames. The first two games were played in Calgary. Edmonton took Game 1 by a score of 3-1. The second game went into overtime, with the teams tied at four goals each. Edmonton was forced to skate one man down during the overtime period, when Mark Messier was sent into the penalty box for two minutes. When a team is a man down they usually are satisfied with "killing" the penalty—that is, getting through the two minutes without having a goal scored against them. But Gretzky did not do things the usual way. Despite being a man down on the ice, Gretzky managed to score the winning goal, a long shot that went over the shoulder of Flames' goalie Mike Vernon, giving the Oilers an overtime victory. It was one of the biggest goals of his career and gave Edmonton a two-game lead over the Flames. At that point the series traveled to Edmonton where the Oilers won two more games and eliminated the Flames.

In the next round Wayne scored four goals and nine assists as the Oilers defeated the Detroit Red Wings in five games. That led to the finals against the Boston Bruins. The Oilers defeated the Bruins in four games straight, but in a roundabout way: Game 4 had to be played twice. The first attempt to play the game—in Boston Gardens, the Bruins' arena—ended in the second period with the score tied 3-3, when there was a power failure that sent everyone home. League rules said that this unfinished game would be tacked on to the end of the series and played only if necessary. The failing lights gave the Oilers an opportunity to win the Stanley Cup on their own ice, which they did. They defeated the Bruins 6-3 and again the Cup was theirs. Of the 21 goals scored by the Oilers in that final series, Gretzky scored or assisted in 13 of them. For the fourth time in five years, Wayne and the Oilers were champions of the NHL.

The "Royal" Wedding

Since Wayne and Janet were often referred to in Canadian newspapers as the "royal couple," it made sense that their July 16, 1988, wedding became known as the "royal wedding." It was held in St. Joseph's Basilica in downtown Edmonton. As Wayne and Janet took their vows, the streets were lined with fans, all straining for a glimpse of the pair as they came out of the church. Fighting for position were press photographers from all over Canada and the United States.

When Wayne and Janet had first announced their engagement, many people in Edmonton disliked seeing their favorite hockey player marry a woman from out of town. But the couple won over the people of Edmonton when they announced that they planned to make the city their home.

Although Wayne and Janet's intentions were good, the couple's future in Edmonton was not to be. Oilers owner Peter Pocklington was having financial trouble and needed to sell some of his most valuable possessions. Other than the team itself, Pocklington's most valuable possession was Wayne.

Janet Jones and Wayne Gretzky, Edmonton's "royal couple," on their wedding day, July 16, 1988 (Associated Press, CP)

6

CALIFORNIA, HERE WE COME

The Gretzkys had been married for less than a month when it was announced that Wayne had been traded to the Los Angeles Kings. Many fans, however, thought that "sold" was a better word for the transaction. Although the Oilers did get several players in return for Gretzky, they were also given $15 million in cash, which went into Peter Pocklington's pocket.

The people of Edmonton were furious. But the Gretzkys, who were by this time expecting their first child, knew the realities of the sports world. Wayne had been sold and it was time to move to Los Angeles. Although Janet had retired as a model and moved all of her belongings to Edmonton, she was happy to be heading back to Los Angeles where she had friends.

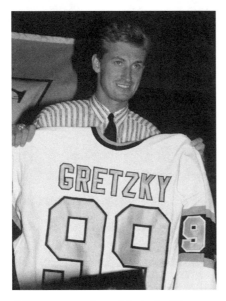

Wayne receives his L.A. Kings jersey. (Bruce Bennett Studios)

On August 9, 1988, during the off-season, the Los Angeles Kings announced that Wayne would be joining as the team captain, and would be wearing his usual number, 99. The Kings' investment in Wayne began to pay dividends right away. Before Gretzky joined the team the Kings sold about 4,000 season tickets, which are tickets that fans buy to attend all home games for the entire season. Once Gretzky became a King, that number jumped to 13,000.

The Kings opened the season at home in front of a sold-out house. Wayne wasted no time making his mark. He scored a goal and had three assists as the Kings defeated the Detroit Red Wings 8-2.

The Hollywood community had not previously paid much attention to the Kings. Basketball had been the "glamour" sport. Now celebrities came out in force to see Wayne. It was no longer unusual to see movie stars sitting behind the Kings' bench.

Wayne and Janet's social life also took a drastic change in Los Angeles. Although Edmonton is a very nice place, it is not known for its glamour. Los Angeles, on the other hand, is overflowing with famous people and affluent lifestyles. For the Gretzkys in southern California, there was now no shortage of invitations to the ritziest parties, and they counted among their friends some of Hollywood's biggest stars of the time, such as Michael J. Fox and John Candy, both of whom were Canadians and hockey fans.

But Wayne and Janet did not let Hollywood glitz slow down their plans for a large family. In 1988 they welcomed their first child, daughter Paulina.

A Changed Team

With Gretzky on the squad, the Kings became the most improved team in the league. They won many more games than they had the previous season. It was clear that, just as had been hoped, Wayne was going to do for the Kings what he had done for the Oilers—instantly transform them into one of the best teams in the league. Los Angeles won 43 games during the 1988–89 season. Because of his passing ability, Wayne made his teammates better players. Bernie Nichols, who frequently shared a shift with Wayne, had scored more than 40 goals in a season twice before, but on the average did not score more than 30. With Wayne feeding him the puck out front of the opponents' nets, Nichols scored 70 goals during the 1988–89 season.

In the first round of the playoffs the Kings had to face Gretzky's old team, the Oilers. Gretzky, still upset about being sold, had no trouble getting psyched for the best-of-seven series. The Kings looked like they were going to exit the playoffs early when they lost three out of the first four games to the Oilers. But it takes four games to win a series, and the Kings buckled down to win the final three games of the series to eliminate the Oilers in seven games. The long series left the Kings exhausted, and they were eliminated in the second round of the playoffs by the Calgary Flames in four straight games.

During that off-season, in August 1989, the Edmonton Oilers (and the people of Edmonton) proved that Wayne would forever be in their hearts. Thousands showed up to see the unveiling of a statue of Wayne that was placed outside the Oilers' arena.

With the new season approaching, the Kings played several preseason games in cities that did not have NHL teams so that fans, who ordinarily would not have had the opportunity, were able to see the great hockey player do his thing.

Breaking Howe's Record

The Kings were playing their sixth game of the 1989–90 season, against the Oilers in Edmonton, when Wayne

Wayne celebrates his 1851st career point with his idol Gordie Howe, who held the previous record of 1850 points. (Bruce Bennett Studios)

scored the 1,851st point of his career. This broke Gordie Howe's career scoring record. The game was stopped and Wayne received a long standing ovation as he was presented with the puck. It had taken Wayne's idol Howe 1,767 games (26 seasons) to do what Wayne had accomplished in 780 games (11 seasons).

The Kings again made it to the playoffs in 1990, but for Wayne the tail end of the season was marred by injuries. In his first game after recovering from a pulled groin muscle, Gretzky was once again injured when the New York Islanders' Alan Kerr checked him from behind. Gretzky ended up missing seven of the last eight regular season games and the first two playoff games. Despite his absence, the Kings defeated the Calgary Flames four games to two. In the second round the Kings went up against the Oilers. Edmonton won four games straight to eliminate the Kings.

Injuries had again troubled Wayne. In the third game versus the Oilers Gretzky was knocked groggy by an early hard hit. He returned only to catch a slap shot in the ear. The resulting cut required 36 stitches to close. It has long been a tradition in hockey that cuts are treated as inconvenient and messy, but certainly nothing serious enough to keep a player out of a game. Many players return to the game as soon as the team doctor is through sewing them up. So no one was surprised when Wayne returned to the game in the third period and scored a goal, but was quickly benched after that because of a sore back. Wayne did not play at all in the final game of the series—which also turned out to be the final game of the Kings' 1990 postseason.

On October 26, 1990, Gretzky passed yet another milestone when he scored his 2,000th career point with an assist against Winnipeg. Wayne scored 41 goals and added 122 assists for a total of 163 points during the 1990–91 season. Three times that season he scored five points in a single game.

During the 1991 playoffs Wayne became the all-time playoff goal leader. Wayne scored four goals and six assists in a six-game series victory over Vancouver in the opening round. That brought on Edmonton and, for the second year in a row, Gretzky's old team eliminated the Kings, this time in six games. Wayne failed to score a goal against the Oilers but did manage five assists.

After the Cold War

The Cold War was a political and cultural battle between democracy and communism that had made nations such as the United States and Canada bitter rivals of the Soviet Union since the end of World War II. The end of the Cold War came in 1990, when the Soviet Union, which was out of money, fell apart into many separate countries. The largest of these was Russia, which was now no longer an archenemy of the countries of the West. With that rivalry out of the way, the biggest competition in international hockey was now between Canada and the United States.

The 1991 Canada Cup gave all hockey fans what they wanted. Following the round-robin portion of the tournament, Canada met the United States in the finals. Unfortunately, Wayne did not get to play a major role in this series. In the first game of the series Wayne was checked hard into the boards from behind. After several moments in which he laid on the ice, Wayne stood up and skated off. But he did not play for the rest of the tournament because of a back injury. Canada went on to win that game 4-1. They won the next game as well, to take the best-of-three series and win the Canada Cup. However, despite missing most of the last two games, Wayne was still the tournament's top scorer.

Walter's Illness

The 1991–92 regular season did not start out well for Wayne either on or off the ice. He played poorly for the first five games of the season. In fact, he was held scoreless over that time. Then came the dreadful news that Wayne's father, Walter, had suffered a brain aneurysm and was near death.

Wayne rushed to be at his father's side. Walter survived, but his memory was forever affected. Today Walter leads a full life and gives inspirational speeches regarding his return from death's door. But sadly, memories of Wayne's greatest victories of the 1980s have been stolen from Walter forever.

Wayne missed five games because of his dad's illness, and when he returned he continued to play poorly. Wayne's play did improve as the season went along and his injured back began to feel better, but the Kings were a middle-of-the-pack team. They gave up more goals than they scored and won only four more than they lost. Los Angeles finished the regular season with a record of 35 wins, 31 losses, and 14 ties. They went to the playoffs but lost in the opening round to Edmonton—the third straight year the Kings had been sent home by the Oilers. Wayne scored two goals and five assists in the six games.

To counter the sadness of that season, there was joy in the Gretzky household as well, as Wayne and Janet's son Ty was born.

Hockey Takes Its Toll

A lifetime of playing hockey takes its toll on the body, even a body as difficult to smash into the boards as Gretzky's. Wayne had missed two or three games here and there after taking tough hits on the ice, but he had never missed a long stretch—until the fall of 1992.

During training camp before the start of the 1992–93 season Wayne's back began to hurt again. In fact, he felt a horrible pain in his back and chest. An MRI showed that Wayne had a herniated disc in his upper spine that was causing pain in his ribs. Wayne ended up missing the first 39 games of the season. He waited until the problem in his spine was completely healed and did not return to action until January 6, 1993.

Even without Gretzky the Kings played better than expected, with 20 wins, 14 losses, and five ties. The Kings' new coach, Barry Melrose, had managed to keep the team focused. In fact, that year the team did better without Wayne than with him. After Gretzky's return the Kings lost more than they won, with a record of 19 wins, 21 losses, and five ties. Over the course of the entire season, the Kings won only four more games than they lost. When the postseason began, fans in Los Angeles had little reason to think that this was a team of Stanley Cup caliber.

It was during the 1992–93 season that Wayne played his 1,000th game in the NHL. He also set another personal record that season, but it was one that he would rather forget: At one point he went 16 straight games without scoring a goal, the longest drought of his career.

Gas in the Tank

The only encouraging aspect of the 1992–93 the season was a factor that no one had considered: Gretzky almost always entered the Stanley Cup playoffs while battling exhaustion. The regular season was long and all hockey players begin to run out of gas as it draws to a close. But this year Wayne had only played less than half of the season and went into the postseason with more "gas in the tank" than most other players. Gretzky was still ready to play.

In the first round the Kings faced Calgary and defeated them in six games. After splitting the first four games, the Kings turned on the offense and scored nine goals each in Games 5 and 6 to win the series. Wayne scored one assist in each of the first three games and was held scoreless in Game 4. In the final two games, however, the Great One turned on the juice, scoring one goal and three assists in

Game 5 and one goal and two assists in Game 6. Gretzky accumulated 10 points in the six-game series.

The Kings then played the Vancouver Canucks and again won in six games. As had been the case in the first round, the Kings and the Canucks split the first four games. The most exciting game of this series for Kings' fans was Game 5, which the Kings won 4-3 in overtime. A 5-3 victory over the Canucks in Game 6 ended the series. Gretzky scored six goals and seven assists against Vancouver.

Playoff fever was growing in Los Angeles. The team that had looked so mediocre during the regular season now moved into the Stanley Cup semifinals against the Toronto Maple Leafs.

In what was getting to be a pattern for the Kings, they split the first four games. The pattern was broken in Game 5, when the Maple Leafs defeated the Kings. That put the Kings in a must-win situation. The fifth game, played in Los Angeles, was an exciting one. Tied after three periods of play,

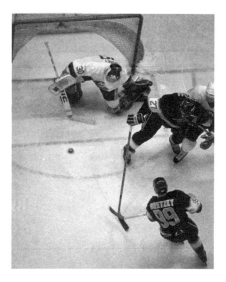

The L.A. Kings' captain, Wayne Gretzky, goes for the goal.
(Bruce Bennett Studios)

Gretzky scored the overtime goal to win the game and tie the series at three games apiece. That brought on the final game of the series, and it would turn out to be what Wayne would call the "best game he had ever played." In the first six games against Toronto Wayne had been relatively quiet on the ice, scoring only one goal and four assists. But in the finale he scored the hat trick and added an assist, as the Kings won the game and the series with a 5-4 victory.

Kings in the Finals

The victory against Toronto put the Kings into the Stanley Cup finals for the first time. Their opponents were the Montreal Canadiens, the team that had won the Cup more often than any other in NHL history. The Canadiens were on a roll. They had won 10 consecutive games in the play-offs. Because of this streak they had played far fewer games to get to the finals than the Kings had, and they were not nearly as tired. On the other hand, the Kings seemed to be a charmed team, a Cinderella story that owed much to Gretzky's joining the team. Despite losing almost as many games as they won during the regular season, the Kings now found themselves only four wins away from their ultimate goal.

That was quickly changed to three wins. The Kings broke Montreal's winning streak in Game 1 of the finals in Montreal, by a score of 4-1. The next three games, however, were all tied after regulation, and Montreal won each of them in overtime. The Canadiens sealed the deal and won the Cup in the fifth game with a 4-1 win in Montreal. Los Angeles' dream run ended. Wayne had been the play-offs' scoring leader with 40 points. During the 1993 post-season he also had become the first NHL player to score 100 goals in the playoffs.

Slip Sliding

The Kings did not improve during the off-season. In fact, they got worse. The 1993–94 regular season was miserable for the Kings. Their record that season was 27 wins, 45 losses, and 12 ties—and they failed to make the postseason. Although Gretzky was again the NHL scoring leader, the Kings played miserably. Wayne had 130 points that season. It would be the last time he would break the 100-point mark

The highlight of the season for Gretzky came on March 23, 1994, when he became the NHL's all-time leading goal scorer. He scored his 802d goal on that night, passing Gordie Howe on the career list. The goal was off goalie Kirk McLean.

The other highlight of the season was the birth of the Gretzkys' third child, son Trevor.

Labor Problems

The 1994–95 NHL season was shortened to 48 games because of labor problems. As had already happened in the professional baseball and football leagues, the union representing the players could not agree with the team owners on fair salary rules. Hockey team owners wanted the players to agree to a salary cap. That is, each team would have a certain amount to spend on players' salaries. If one player—such as Wayne, for example—made a lot of money, the other players on the team would have to make less so that the entire roster could stay "under the cap." In this manner, the team owners with the most money would not be able to dominate the league by buying up all the best players.

But the players said no to the salary cap, and the first two months of the season were canceled. Unlike other sports, this was not a strike because the players wanted to play. The players were "locked out" of the arenas by owners who were preventing them from playing, so the term for the stoppage was lockout.

Eventually, the owners gave in. There would be no salary cap. However, in return for that, the players agreed that they could not become free agents until they turned 32 years old. That meant that players had to play for the team that drafted them, or for the team they were traded to, until that age. After that a player would be able to play for the team that agreed to pay him the most money. The average length of a pro hockey career was five years. Most hockey players would be out of the game by the time they were 32 years old. That meant that only a few players would ever have the opportunity to become free agents.

It is unclear who won the labor dispute. Neither the owners nor the players were happy. But the biggest losers were the fans, who missed out on two months of hockey.

The Ninety-Nine All-Stars

During the lockout, Wayne was not content to just take a vacation. He was only really happy when he was playing hockey, so he organized an NHL All-Star team. He called them the Ninety-Nine All-Stars, after his jersey number.

The Ninety-Nine All-Stars tour (Bruce Bennett Studios)

They toured Europe, playing various European teams. All the money raised from these games went to charity. To keep things in the family, Wayne's dad, Walter, was the coach. Most of the games were held in Germany, Finland, and Sweden, where hockey was very popular. The NHL stars spent hours signing autographs for the European fans, who showed up at the games in unexpectedly large numbers.

When NHL exhibition games finally started, Wayne arranged for players from opposing teams to shake hands on the ice before the start of the game. This showed the fans that all the players were united against the owners. Regular-season games did not start until January 1995.

Kings Go Bankrupt

Just as Peter Pocklington, owner of the Edmonton franchise, had experienced financial difficulties when Wayne played for the Oilers, the owner of the Kings, Bruce McNall, had money problems when Wayne was on his team. During the 1995 season, McNall, badly in debt, filed for bankruptcy.

To make matters even worse, the Kings were a bad team. It was proved that Wayne could not single-handedly win hockey games anymore. Without the supporting cast that a strong team provides, Wayne's presence on the ice was wasted. The Kings only won 11 games in 1995. For the second year in a row, Los Angeles was one of the few teams to not make it to the playoffs.

It was Wayne's eighth year playing in Los Angeles, and his contract was up. His owner was in debt. It was clear that Wayne's days as a King were just about over.

Meet Me in St. Louis

During the 1995–96 season the Kings were in a rebuilding mode. Bruce McNall was leaving the team's front office, so Wayne felt like it was also time for him to move on. On February 27, 1996, Wayne got his wish. He was traded to the St. Louis Blues. In return the Kings got three players and two future draft choices. At the time Shayne Corson was the captain of the Blues, but he immediately gave up the job to Wayne, so Gretzky became captain of his third NHL team.

It was a happy move for Wayne—at least at first. In St. Louis he could be a teammate of his friend Brett Hull, a superstar in his own right and son of the legendary Bobby Hull. To make matters even happier for Gretzky, the team was coached by Mike Keenan, for whom Wayne had played on Team Canada in the 1987 and 1991 Canada Cup games.

But Wayne's career with the Blues got off to a rocky start. In his second game he was knocked unconscious by an elbow thrown by Edmonton Oiler Kelly Buchberger. Gretzky suffered a mild concussion. Later in the season Wayne was injured again, this time when he was checked

Wayne's brief time with the St. Louis Blues was a low point in his career. (Bruce Bennett Studios)

by Toronto's Doug Gilmour, and suffered a deep bruise in his back when he fell hard to the ice. The Blues played well enough to make the playoffs, however.

That year the Blues defeated the Toronto Maple Leafs in the first round of the playoffs. The Blues won the series four games to two. Wayne failed to score a single goal against the Maple Leafs, but he did contribute nine assists. St. Louis faced the Detroit Red Wings in the second round and lost in seven games. Gretzky did not play his best, scoring only two goals and five assists. One point per game would be an excellent average for any other player, but not for the Great One. He was starting to show his age. He was slower than anyone had seen him, and twice, when the Red Wings had the puck, he lost his man who went on to score a goal. While others tried to sugar coat the matter, Wayne did not. "I stink," he said.

Apparently, the Blues' front office agreed with Wayne's opinion. They took an offer for a long-term contract off the table. Wayne declared himself a free agent and put himself on the open market. He didn't know who he was going to play for during the 1996–97 season, but he knew it wouldn't be the Blues.

7

LAST DAYS IN THE BIG APPLE

On July 21, 1996, Wayne signed as a free agent with the New York Rangers, whose home arena is Madison Square Garden. He had previously known the glare of being in the media spotlight while playing in Los Angeles, but that had been nothing compared to the public attention he received while playing in the Big Apple, the media capital of the world. It is unfortunate that New York only got to see Gretzky play for the Rangers during the final years of his career, when his skills had sadly eroded. Still, he received the superstar treatment everywhere he went. Being a Ranger also made him once again a teammate of Mark Messier, with whom he had won four Stanley Cups in Edmonton.

In August of 1996, before Wayne had a chance to play his first game as a Ranger, he played in the World Cup—the hockey tournament formerly known as the Canada Cup. The games were played in Montreal and, to the surprise of no one, Wayne was the captain of Team Canada.

The tournament gave Gretzky the opportunity to play on the same team as Messier for the first time in eight years. Wayne and Mark would have an opportunity to get reacquainted before the start of that year's Rangers' season. Adding to the nostalgic feel of the event was Glen Sather, the coach of Team Canada who had been Gretzky and Messier's coach during their Oiler glory years.

Sather put Gretzky and Messier on the same line, saying, "They looked like they wanted to play together. They were like a couple of teenagers . . . like a couple of brothers who hadn't seen each other in a long, long time."

In eight games of international play Gretzky scored only six points (three goals, three assists), and Team Canada lost in the finals to its new arch rival, the United States. Canada and the U.S. played a best-of-three series in the finals. After splitting the first two games, Canada took a 2-1 lead into the third period before giving up four straight goals and the championship in the final minutes.

Madison Square Garden Days

Gretzky's first year as a Ranger was his best. On December 1, 1996, during a game versus Montreal, Wayne scored his 3,000th point. He played in all 82 regular season games, scoring 97 points (25 goals, 72 assists), the most he had scored since the 1993–94 season.

The Rangers made the playoffs and performed well in the postseason. They defeated Florida in five games and New Jersey in five before losing to the Philadelphia Flyers, also in five games. Wayne played solid hockey throughout the postseason, scoring 20 points in 15 games.

Wayne fires a slap shot for the New York Rangers. (Bruce Bennett Studios)

That was the high point for Wayne as a Ranger. He would never play another postseason game. Although Wayne played two more full seasons with the Rangers, neither was very good and in neither did the team come close to making the playoffs.

A Bad Night for Janet

Wayne wasn't the only Gretzky who was hit during Rangers' games in the 1997–98 season. On October 22, 1997, in Madison Square Garden, during a game in which the New York Rangers were playing Chicago, a play against the boards dislodged the Plexiglas designed to protect the crowd. The protective sheet crashed down onto the front rows and knocked a woman unconscious.

As players skated over to the scene of the accident, they were shocked to see that the woman was Wayne's wife, Janet Gretzky, who had been sitting in the front row. Janet suffered a mild concussion and a small cut on her lip.

Wayne was clearly upset by the accident, but stayed with his team as Janet was taken to St. Luke's-Roosevelt Hospital. Another woman sitting close to Janet also appeared to be injured but did not require treatment at the hospital.

The game was halted for 10 minutes before play resumed. As soon as the game was over, Wayne rushed to the hospital to be at Janet's side. The Rangers had lost the game 1-0 to the Chicago Blackhawks.

On the ice Wayne's numbers were shrinking. In 1997–98 he scored 90 points, with 23 goals and 67 assists. The following year, his last, he missed 12 games due to injury and saw his productivity slip to nine goals and 53 assists, for a total of 62 points.

The Order of Canada Medal

In January 1998 Wayne received the Order of Canada medal to honor his contributions to hockey. Governor General Romeo LeBlanc gave Wayne the medal at a ceremony at Rideeau Hall in Ottawa. Gretzky had actually received the honor back in 1984 but, because the ceremonies were always held during hockey games, it had taken him nearly 14 years to receive his medal. "To be standing here today in Ottawa receiving this award is something I'll never forget. I'm very proud to be Canadian," said Gretzky.

After the ceremony Wayne told the assembled reporters that he hoped to be wearing another medal soon—a gold medal, which he hoped to win at the upcoming Olympics. In 1998 Wayne played for Team Canada at the Winter Olympics in Nagano, Japan.

Unfortunately, Team Canada had a disappointing performance in the '98 Olympics. In the semifinals Canada lost to the Czech Republic, and then in the consolation game to see who won the third-place bronze medal, Canada lost again, this time to Finland. In six Olympic games, Gretzky scored no goals and managed only four assists.

At the 1999 National Hockey League All-Star game, held in Tampa Bay, Florida, Wayne won the Most Valuable Player Award, becoming the only hockey player to ever win that award in his last year in the league. Gretzky's most memorable play of the game was a pinpoint centering pass to Mark Recchi that led to a Team North America goal.

Final Curtain

The first public suggestion that Gretzky's hockey career was nearing an end came on April 10, 1999, when John Davidson, the former goalie and TV hockey announcer, said on the air in Canada that Gretzky was thinking about retirement. When the press asked Gretzky about Davidson's statement, he refused to deny it. So on April 15, 1999, when Gretzky arrived at the Ottawa Senators' arena for the team's scheduled game against the New York Rangers, hockey fans across Canada knew it was to be Gretzky's last game in Canada.

As if to confirm a statement that Gretzky had yet to make, the Senators invited Wayne's entire family to the game. The crowd arrived early that night. The seats were filled an hour before the game started to see Gretzky go through his pregame warm-ups one last time. Then fans

The Great One waves to his fans after his final game.
(Bruce Bennett Studios)

lowered their eyes when they heard Gretzky had scheduled a press conference after the game. He had an announcement to make.

Fans brought signs to the game. "Say it ain't so, Wayne," one read.

After the game the Senators lined up on the ice and each team member shook hands with the greatest hockey player of them all. At the postgame press conference Gretzky came just short of announcing his retirement. That would be done after his final game, three days later, in New York. However, he did say that when it came to retirement, "All indications are obviously pointing in that direction. Obviously, it is an emotional time for me. It's an experience I'll never forget, tonight."

On April 18, 1999, Gretzky played his last game, a 2-1 overtime loss to the Pittsburgh Penguins. The Madison Square Garden ice had been freshly decorated for the occasion, with a big "99" painted on the ice behind each goal. During the game Gretzky scored one assist, the final point of his record-setting scoring career, but he was sitting on the bench at the end of the game when the Penguins scored the winning goal.

"This is a celebration."

Gretzky finally made it official after the game, at a press conference in Madison Square Garden.

"Unfortunately," he said, "sometimes you go to funerals, and fortunately sometimes you go to weddings and fun parties. And to me, this is a party. This is a celebration. I hope everyone understands that I look upon these next few days as something to really enjoy. It's obvious that today I have officially retired. In my heart, I know I made the right decision. My gut, my heart is telling me this is the right time. A year from now, I could be in the exact same situation, with everyone saying I should play one more year. I'm done. I have not wavered at all and I will not play again."

In his final game Gretzky used 51 different sticks. He then signed each of them and gave them away to his teammates and friends.

Hall of Fame

Hockey players generally wait three years after they play their final game before being considered for induction into the Hockey Hall of Fame. However, on April 29, 1999, just days after Wayne announced his retirement, the Hockey Hall of Fame's selection committee decided to waive the three-year waiting period in Gretzky's case.

As a kid Wayne had frequently visited the Hall of Fame building in Toronto. "I would stand there and stare at all the pictures, the sweaters and the hockey sticks. I could never go in there enough. I never thought that one day I'd have the opportunity to be in the Hall of Fame. But dreams, I guess, come true." He was officially inducted into the Hall of Fame on November 22, 1999.

Gretzky biographer Scott Morrison points out that Gretzky's greatness on the ice is really only part of the story: "Gretzky is a magnificent person and a great Canadian." This is exemplified by "his thoughtfulness, his humble nature, his compassion, his remarkable attention to detail, the way he makes sure the right thing and the right person are always taken care of."

Shortly after Wayne's retirement the Gretzkys moved back to Los Angeles. And in early 2000 Janet gave birth to their fourth child, Tristan.

Gretzky Since Retirement

With Wayne retired he was no longer on the road for most of the year, and the Gretzkys had their first chance to settle down. They built a large house on top of an eight-acre hill in California. The house is full of dogs (four dachshunds) and kids. With the addition of daughter Emma in 2003, there are now five Gretzky children. "We're trying to form some roots here," said Janet, not long after Wayne's retirement. "Being a professional hockey player, you tend to move around. It's not as if there's a probability of Wayne wanting to go back to Brantford. It's not as if I'm thinking of going back to St. Louis [where she grew up]. We're a young family and we have to find our own roots and it seems to be California. Wayne likes the West Coast. We live in a great neighborhood. It's very family-oriented and clean. There's good weather all year round. You can play sports all year round, so probably for a while, we'll be here."

From the Ice to the Front Office

Even though Wayne is done playing hockey for a living, he has not left the sport behind. The game will always be a big part of his life. On June 2, 2000, Gretzky made his debut as an NHL front-office man: He became a managing partner in charge of hockey operations for the Phoenix Coyotes. It is Gretzky's job to transform the Coyotes into one of the league's top teams, a position it did not enjoy when Wayne signed on.

In 2002 Wayne served as the Executive Director of Team Canada's Olympic Hockey Team and was responsible for assembling Canada's best ice hockey players at the 2002 Olympic Winter Games in Salt Lake City. He did a great job, too. Team Canada won the Olympic Gold Medal for the first time since 1952. During the Olympics that year Wayne was further honored. He received the Olympic Order, the highest honor that can be given by the International Olympic Committee, for his "outstanding contributions to the game of hockey."

Wayne is a regular on TV commercials and advertisements of all sorts. Among the corporations he has agreed to represent are McDonald's Canada, Anheuser-Busch, Hudson's Bay Co., Imperial Oil, and Ford Canada.

In March 2003 Gretzky was given one of the great honors that can be bestowed upon a sports figure: A portrait of Wayne was placed on the cover of the Wheaties breakfast-cereal box. The cover of the orange box is a spot reserved for only the very best athletes. Previous stars to appear on the Wheaties box include golf's Tiger Woods and legendary boxing champion Muhammad Ali.

The following month Wayne was given the inaugural International Horatio Alger Award at ceremonies at the U.S. State Department in Washington, D.C. (Horatio Alger is a fictional character who became a symbol for great achievement following humble beginnings.) Among the members of the Horatio Alger Association are award-winning poet Dr. Maya Angelou, former Senator Robert J.

Dole, boxing legend George Foreman, Reverend Billy Graham, Secretary of State Colin Powell, and celebrity media figure Oprah Winfrey. Walter Scott Jr., president of the association, said, "Wayne Gretzky has proven what the rewards of hard work, determination, and positive thinking are through his incredible professional and personal achievements."

In the winter months Wayne is busy with the Wayne Gretzky Fantasy Camp held each February in Scottsdale, Arizona. For five days lucky campers, all of whom are adults over 21, skate with Gretzky and other NHL stars and celebrities. They take lessons in hockey techniques and play games alongside the legends. A portion of the proceeds from the fantasy camp go to the Wayne Gretzky Foundation, a charitable organization that helps disadvantaged youngsters participate in hockey.

Charity Work

Since his retirement Gretzky has been more involved than ever in raising funds for charity. During the summer of 2003 Wayne helped raise $400,000 for children's charities and Calgary's Ronald McDonald House. He did it by inviting his celebrity friends, both from the worlds of sports and show business, to the three-day Ronald McDonald Children's Charities Wayne Gretzky and Friends Golf Invitational.

The Ronald McDonald House is not the only charity work fund-raising that Wayne does. He is chairman of the Esso Medals of Achievement Program, which provides medals and certificates to young, nonprofessional hockey players. He is an Athlete Ambassador and Honorary Member of the Board of Trustees of Olympic Aid, an athlete-driven humanitarian organization that uses sports to enhance child development in some of the most disadvantaged communities in the world.

The Babe Ruth of Hockey

It has been said that Wayne Gretzky was the Babe Ruth of hockey. Babe Ruth was the baseball player who practically invented the home run as an offensive weapon. While he was playing from the 1910s until the 1930s, most of the records he broke were his own. At that time people thought the Babe's records would never be broken. But times change, and after two generations of ballplayers, eventually he was surpassed.

Today's hockey fans feel much the same way about Gretzky as baseball fans felt about Babe Ruth in his day. Although Wayne's records might stand for years to come, there may be an as-yet-unknown young hockey player out there who has what it takes to set even more impressive records than the Great One.

(Bruce Bennett Studios)

But scores aside, it was Wayne Gretzky's unique playing style, good-natured personality, and genuine love of the game that made him the unique athlete that hockey and sports fans of all types will never forget. That is a record that cannot be broken.

TIME LINE

Lines with two years represent a hockey season.

1961 Born on January 26 in Brantford, Ontario

1978 Signs first big-league hockey contract with the
Indianapolis Racers of the World Hockey
Association (WHA); traded to the Edmonton Oilers,
then of the WHA

1979 Scores his first NHL assist, setting up teammate
Kevin Lowe in a game in Chicago; scores first career
goal, against Vancouver

1979– Edmonton Oilers become NHL team, largely out of
1980 NHL's desire to have Gretzky as a player

1980 Plays in first of 18 NHL All-Star games (1980–86,
1988–94, and 1996–99); records seven assists in one
game, an NHL record tied only by himself on
December 11, 1985, and February 14, 1986; becomes

youngest NHL player (19 years, two months) ever to score 50 goals in a season; wins first of four Lady Byng trophies (1979–80, 1990–91, 1991–92, and 1993–94); wins first of nine Hart Memorial trophies (1979–80 through 1986–87 and 1988–89)

1981   Named NHL Player of Year by *The Sporting News,* an award he won seven times (1980–81 through 1986–87); also wins first of 10 Art Ross memorial trophies, awarded to the NHL leading scorer (1980–81 through 1986–87, 1989–90, 1990–91, and 1993–94)

1982   Sets NHL record by scoring 92 goals during the 1981–82 season; also scores more than 200 points (total goals and assists) during the season for the first of four times in his career and scores a record 10 hat tricks (three goals in a game)

1983   Sets an All-Star game record by scoring four goals in one period and is named captain of the Oilers

1983–   Scores a point in a record 51 consecutive games
1984

1984   Records 1,000th point of his career versus Los Angeles

1985   Leads Oilers to their first Stanley Cup championship, the first of four he won with the club

1985– Sets NHL single-season records with 215 points and
1986   163 assists

1988   Marries model and actress Janet Jones in
            Edmonton; traded to Los Angeles Kings; named
            team captain

1994   Passes Gordie Howe to become the NHL's all-time
            leading scorer

1996   In February, traded to St. Louis Blues and named
            team captain; in July, signed as a free agent by the
            New York Rangers

1998   Plays for Team Canada in the Winter Olympics

1999   Plays final game of career, a 2-1 overtime loss to the
            Pittsburgh Penguins; records one final assist;
            announces retirement; inducted into the Hockey
            Hall of Fame

HOW TO BECOME A PROFESSIONAL ATHLETE

THE JOB

Unlike amateur athletes who play or compete in amateur circles for titles or trophies only, professional athletic teams compete against one another to win titles, championships, and series; team members are paid salaries and bonuses for their work.

The athletic performances of individual teams are evaluated according to the nature and rules of each specific sport: Usually the winning team compiles the highest score, as in football, basketball, and soccer. Competitions are organized by local, regional, national, and international organizations and associations, whose primary functions are to promote the sport and sponsor competitive events. Within a professional sport there are usually different levels of competition based on age, ability, and gender. There are often different designations and divisions within one sport. Professional baseball, for example, is made up of the two major leagues (American and National) each made up of three divisions, East, Central, and West, and the minor leagues (single-A, double-A, triple-A). All of these teams are considered professional because the players are compensated for their work, but the financial rewards are the greatest in the major leagues.

Whatever the team sport, most team members specialize in a specific area of the game. In gymnastics, for example, the entire six-member team trains on all of the gymnastic apparatuses—balance beam, uneven bars, vault, and floor exercise—but usually each of the six gymnasts excels in only one or two areas. Those gymnasts who do excel in all four events are likely to do well in the individual, all-around title, which is a part of the team competition. Team members in football, basketball, baseball, soccer, and hockey all assume different positions, some of which change depending on whether or not the team is trying to score a goal (offensive positions) or prevent the opposition from scoring one (defensive positions). During team practices, athletes focus on their specific role in a game, whether that is defensive, offensive, or both. For example, a pitcher will spend some time running bases and throwing to other positions, but the majority of his or her time will most likely be spent practicing pitching.

Professional teams train for most of the year, but unlike athletes in individual sports, the athletes who are members of a team usually have more of an off-season. Professional athletes' training programs differ according to the season. Following an off-season, most team sports have a training season in which they begin to increase the intensity of their workouts after a period of relative inactivity, in order to develop or maintain strength, cardiovascular ability, flexibility, endurance, speed, and quickness, as well as to focus on technique and control. During the season the team coach, physician, trainers, and physical therapists organize specific routines, programs, or exercises to target game skills as well as individual athletic weaknesses, whether skill-related or from injury.

These workouts also vary according to the difficulty of the game schedule. During a playoff or championship series, the coach and athletic staff realize that a rigorous workout in between games might tax the athletes' strength, stamina, or even mental preparedness, jeopardizing the outcome of the next game. Instead, the coach might prescribe a mild workout followed by intensive stretching. In addition to stretching and exercising the specific muscles used in any given sport, athletes concentrate on developing excellent eating and sleeping habits that will help them remain in top condition throughout the year. Abstaining from drinking alcoholic beverages during a season is a practice to which many professional athletes adhere.

The coaching or training staff often films the games and practices so that the team can benefit from watching their individual exploits, as well as their combined play. By watching their performances, team members can learn how to improve their techniques and strategies. It is common for professional teams to also study other teams' moves and strategies in order to determine a method of coping with the other teams' plays during a game.

REQUIREMENTS
High School

Most professional athletes demonstrate tremendous skill and interest in their sport well before high school. High school offers student athletes the opportunity to gain experience in the field in a structured and competitive environment. Under the guidance of a coach, you can begin developing suitable training programs and learn about health, nutrition, and conditioning issues.

High school also offers you the opportunity to experiment with a variety of sports and a variety of positions within a sport. Most junior varsity and some varsity high school teams allow you to try out different positions and begin to discover whether you have more of an aptitude for the defensive dives of a goalie or for the forwards' front-line action. High school coaches will help you learn to expand upon your strengths and abilities and develop yourself more fully as an athlete. High school is also an excellent time to begin developing the concentration powers, leadership skills, and good sportsmanship necessary for success on the field.

People who hope to become professional athletes should take a full load of high school courses including four years of English, math, and science, as well as health and physical education. A solid high school education will help ensure success in college (often the next step in becoming a professional athlete) and may help you earn a college athletic scholarship. A high school diploma will certainly give you something to fall back on if an injury, a change in career goals, or other circumstance prevents you from earning a living as an athlete.

Postsecondary Training

College is important for future professional athletes for several reasons. It provides the opportunity to gain skill and strength in your sport before you try to succeed in the pros, and it also offers you the chance of being observed by professional scouts.

Perhaps most importantly, a college education provides you with a valuable degree that you can use if you do not earn a living as a professional athlete or after your professional career ends. College athletes major in everything from communications to pre-med and enjoy careers as coaches, broadcasters, teachers, doctors, actors, and businesspeople, to name a few. As with high school sports, college athletes must maintain certain academic standards in order to be permitted to compete in intercollegiate play.

Other Requirements

If you want to be a professional athlete, you must be fully committed to succeeding. You must work almost nonstop to improve your conditioning and skills, and not give up when you don't succeed as quickly or as easily as you had hoped. And even then, because the competition is so fierce, the goal of earning a living as a professional athlete is still difficult to reach. For this reason, professional athletes must not get discouraged easily. They must have the self-confidence and ambition to keep working and keep trying. Professional athletes also must have a love for their sport that compels them to want to reach their fullest potential.

EXPLORING

Students interested in pursuing a career in professional sports should start playing that sport as much and as early as possible. Most junior high and high schools have well-established programs in the sports that are played at the professional level.

If a team sport does not exist in your school that does not mean your chances of playing it have evaporated. Petition your school board to establish it as a school sport and set aside funds for it. In the meantime organize other students into a club team, scheduling practices and unofficial games. If the sport is a recognized team sport in the United States or Canada, contact the sport's professional organization for additional information; if anyone would have helpful tips for gaining recognition, the professional organization would. Also, try calling the local or state athletic board to see whether or not any other schools in your area recognize it as a team sport, and make a list of those teams and try scheduling exhibition games with them. Your goal is to show your school or school board that other students have a definite interest in the game and that other schools recognize it.

To determine if you really want to commit to pursuing a professional career in your team sport, talk to coaches, trainers, and any athletes who are currently pursuing a professional career. You can also contact professional organizations and associations for information on how to best prepare for a career in their sport. Sometimes there are specialized training programs available, and the best way to find out is to get in contact with the people whose job it is to promote the sport.

EMPLOYERS

Professional athletes are employed by private and public ownership groups throughout the United States and Canada. At the highest male professional level, there are 32 National Football League franchises, 30 Major League Baseball franchises, 29 National Basketball Association franchises, 30 National Hockey League franchises, and 10 Major League Soccer franchises. The Women's National Basketball Association has 16 franchises.

STARTING OUT

Most team sports have some official manner of establishing which teams acquire which players; often this is referred to as a draft, although sometimes members of a professional team are chosen through a competition. Usually the draft occurs between the college and professional levels of the sport. The National Basketball Association (NBA), for example, has its NBA College Draft. During the draft the owners and managers of professional basketball teams choose players in an order based on the team's performance in the previous season. This means that the team with the worst record in the previous season has a greater chance of getting to choose first from the list of available players.

Furthermore, professional athletes must meet the requirements established by the organizing bodies of their respective sport. Sometimes this means meeting a physical requirement, such as age, height, and weight; and sometimes this means fulfilling a number of required stunts, or participating in a certain number of competitions. Professional organizations usually arrange it so that athletes can build up their skills and level of play by participating in lower-level competitions. College sports, as mentioned before, are an excellent way to improve one's skills while pursuing an education.

ADVANCEMENT

Professional athletes in team sports advance in three ways: when their team advances, when they are traded to better teams, and when they negotiate better contracts. In all three instances, the individual team member who works and practices hard, and who gives his or her best performance in game after game achieves this. Winning teams also receive a deluge of media attention that often creates celebrities out of individual players, which in turn provides these top players with opportunities for financially rewarding commercial endorsements.

Professional athletes are usually represented by *sports agents* in the behind-the-scenes deals that determine for which teams they will be playing and what they will be paid. These agents may also be involved with other key decisions involving commercial endorsements, personal income taxes, and financial investments of the athlete's revenues.

In the moves from high school athletics to collegiate athletics and from collegiate athletics to the pros, coaches and scouts are continually scouring the ranks of high school and college teams for new talent; they're most interested in the athletes who consistently deliver points or prevent the opposition from scoring. There is simply no substitute for success.

A college education, however, can prepare all athletes for the day when their bodies can no longer compete at the top level, whether because of age or an unforeseen injury. Every athlete should be prepared to move into another career, whether it is related to the world of sports or not.

Professional athletes do have other options, especially those who have graduated from a four-year college or university. Many go into some area of coaching, sports administration, management, or broadcasting. The professional athlete's unique insight and perspective can be a real asset in these careers. Other athletes simultaneously pursue other interests, some completely unrelated to their sport, such as education, business, social welfare, or the arts. Many continue to stay involved with the sport they have loved since childhood, coaching young children or volunteering with local school teams.

EARNINGS

Today professional athletes who are members of top-level teams earn hundreds of thousands of dollars in prize money at professional competitions; the top players or athletes in each sport earn as much or more in endorsements and advertising, usually for sports-related products and services, but increasingly for products or services completely unrelated to their sport. Such salaries and other incomes are not representative of the whole field of professional athletes, but are only indicative of the fantastic revenues a few rare athletes with extraordinary talent can hope to earn. In 2000 athletes had median annual earnings of $43,370, according to the U.S. Department of Labor. Ten percent earned less than $13,610.

Perhaps the only caveat to the financial success of an elite athlete is the individual's character or personality. An athlete with a bad temper or who is prone to unsportsmanlike behavior may still be able to participate in team play, helping to win games and garner trophies, but he or she won't necessarily be able to cash in on the commercial endorsements. Advertisers are notoriously fickle about the spokespeople they choose to endorse products;

some athletes have lost million-dollar accounts because of their bad behavior on and off the court.

WORK ENVIRONMENT

Athletes compete in many different conditions, according to the setting of the sport (indoors or outdoors) and the rules of the organizing or governing bodies. Athletes who participate in football or soccer, for example, often compete in hot, rainy, or freezing conditions, but at any point, organizing officials can call off the match, or postpone competition until better weather.

Indoor events are less subject to cancellation. However, since it is in the best interests of an organization not to risk the athletes' health, any condition that might adversely affect the outcome of a competition is usually reason to cancel or postpone it. The coach or team physician, on the other hand, may withdraw an athlete from a game if that athlete is injured or ill. Nerves and fear are not good reasons to default on a competition, and part of ascending into the ranks of professional athletes means learning to cope with the anxiety that comes with competition. Some athletes, however, actually thrive on the nervous tension.

In order to reach the elite level of any sport, athletes must begin their careers early. Most professional athletes have been honing their skills since they were quite young. Athletes fit hours of practice time into an already full day;

many famous players practiced on their own before school, as well as for several hours after school during team practice. Competitions are often far from the young athlete's home, which means they must travel on a bus or in a van with the team and coaching staff. Sometimes young athletes are placed in special training programs far from their homes and parents. They live with other athletes training for the same sport or on the same team and only see their parents for holidays and vacations. The separation from a child's parents and family can be difficult; often an athlete's family decides to move in order to be closer to the child's training facility.

The expenses of a sport can be overwhelming, as is the time an athlete must devote to practice and travel to and from competitions. Although most high school athletic programs pay for many expenses, if the athlete wants additional training or private coaching, the child's parents must come up with the extra money. Sometimes young athletes can get official sponsors or they might qualify for an athletic scholarship from the training program. In addition to specialized equipment and clothing, the athlete must sometimes pay for a coach, travel expenses, competition fees, and, depending on the sport, time at the facility or gym where he or she practices. Gymnasts, for example, train for years as individuals, and then compete for positions on national or international teams. Up until the time they are accepted (and usually during their participation in the team), these gymnasts must pay for their expenses—from coach to travel to uniforms to room and board away from home.

Even with the years of hard work, practice, and financial sacrifice that most athletes and their families must endure, there is no guarantee that an athlete will achieve the rarest of the rare in the sports world—financial reward. An athlete needs to truly love the sport at which he or she excels, and also have a nearly insatiable ambition and work ethic.

OUTLOOK

The outlook for professional athletes will vary depending on the sport, its popularity, and the number of positions open with professional teams. On the whole, the outlook for the field of professional sports is healthy, but the number of jobs will not increase dramatically. Some sports, however, may experience a rise in popularity, which may translate into greater opportunities for higher salaries, prize monies, and commercial endorsements.

TO LEARN MORE ABOUT PROFESSIONAL ATHLETES

BOOKS

Coffey, Wayne. *Carl Lewis: The Triumph of Discipline*. Woodbridge, Conn.: Blackbirch Press, 1992.

Freedman, Russell. *Babe Didrikson Zaharias*. New York: Clarion, 1999.

Krull, Kathleen. *Lives of the Athletes: Thrills, Spills (and What the Neighbors Thought)*. New York: Harcourt Brace, 1997.

Rudeen, Kenneth. *Jackie Robinson*. New York: HarperTrophy, 1996.

Stewart, Mark. *Tiger Woods: Driving Force*. Danbury, Conn.: Children's Press, 1998.

Updyke, Rosemary Kissinger. *Jim Thorpe, the Legend Remembered*. New York: Pelican, 1997.

ORGANIZATIONS

Young people who are interested in becoming professional athletes should contact the professional organizations for the sport in which they would like to compete, such as the National Hockey League, U.S. Tennis Association, the Professional Golfer's Association, or the National Bowling Association. Ask for information on requirements, training centers, coaches, and so on.

For a free brochure and information on the Junior Olympics and more, write to
Amateur Athletic Union
C/o The Walt Disney World Resort
P.O. Box 10000
Lake Buena Vista, FL 32830-1000
www.aausports.org

For additional information on athletics, contact
American Alliance for Health, Physical Education, Recreation, and Dance
1900 Association Drive
Reston, VA 20191
www.aahperd.org

The popular magazine *Sports Illustrated for Kids* also has a website.

Sports Illustrated for Kids

www.sikids.com

Visit the U.S. Olympic Committee's website for the latest sporting news and information about upcoming Olympic competitions.

United States Olympic Committee

www.olympic-usa.org

The following website provides information about and links to women in all kinds of sports:

Women in Sports

www.makeithappen.com/wis/index.html

TO LEARN MORE ABOUT WAYNE GRETZKY AND HOCKEY

BOOKS

Cady, Steve, et al. *High-Performance Skating for Hockey*. Champaign, Ill.: Human Kinetics, 1998.

Chambers, Dave. *Complete Hockey Instruction: Skills and Strategies for Coaches and Players*. New York: Contemporary Books, 1994.

——. *The Incredible Hockey Drill Book*. New York: Contemporary Books, 1995.

Christopher, Matt. *On the Ice with Wayne Gretzky*. New York: Little, Brown, 1996.

Fortunato, Frank. *Wayne Gretzky: Star Center*. Berkeley Heights, N.J.: Enslow Publishers, 1998.

Gretzky, Walter, and Jim Taylor. *Gretzky: From Backyard Rink to the Stanley Cup*. New York: Avon Books, 1985.

Jones, Terry. *The Great Gretzky Yearbook*. Toronto: General Paperbacks, 1981.

Kramer, S. A. *The Great Gretzky*, New York: Grosset & Dunlap, 2000.

Morrison, Scott. *Wayne Gretzky: The Great Goodbye*. Toronto: Firefly Books, 1999.

Podnieks, Andrew. *The Great One: The Life and Times of Wayne Gretzky*. Chicago: Triumph Books, 1999.

Raber, Thomas R. *Wayne Gretzky: Hockey Great*. Minneapolis: First Avenue Editions, 1999.

Redmond, Gerald. *Wayne Gretzky: The Great One*. Toronto: ECW Press, 1993.

Santella, Andrew, *Wayne Gretzky: The Great One*. New York: Franklin Watts Inc., 1999.

Stamm, Laura, and Herb Brooks. *Power Skating*. Champaign, Ill.: Human Kinetics, 2001.

Twist, Peter, and Pavel Bure. *Complete Conditioning for Ice Hockey*. Champaign, Ill.: Human Kinetics, 1996.

NEWSPAPERS AND MAGAZINES

Kates, Brian. "Holy Grail: The Honus Wagner T206." *Daily News*, June 22, 2003, p. 51.

LeRoux, Jacki. "Gretzky Receives Order of Canada," *Ottawa Sun*, January 29, 1998, p. 3.

Strachen, Al. "Janet and the Kids Looking Forward to Having Dad at Home," *Toronto Sun*, November 22, 1999, p. 5.

WEBSITES

Hockey Hall of Fame

www.hhof.com

National Hockey League

www.nhl.com

USA Hockey

www.usahockey.com

World Hockey Association

www.worldhockeyassociation.net

WAYNE GRETZKY'S CAREER STATS

YEAR	TEAM	GM	G	A	PTS
1979–80	Edmonton	79	51	86	137
1980–81	Edmonton	80	55	109	164
1981–82	Edmonton	80	92	120	212
1982–83	Edmonton	80	71	125	196
1983–84	Edmonton	74	87	118	205
1984–85	Edmonton	80	73	135	208
1985–86	Edmonton	80	52	163	215
1986–87	Edmonton	79	62	121	183
1987–88	Edmonton	64	40	109	149

YEAR	TEAM	GM	G	A	PTS
1988–89	Los Angeles	78	54	114	168
1989–90	Los Angeles	73	40	102	142
1990–91	Los Angeles	78	41	122	163
1991–92	Los Angeles	74	31	90	121
1992–93	Los Angeles	45	16	49	65
1993–94	Los Angeles	81	38	92	130
1994–95	Los Angeles	48	11	37	48
1995–96	Los Angeles	62	15	66	81
	St. Louis	18	8	13	21
1996–97	NY Rangers	82	25	72	97
1997–98	NY Rangers	82	23	67	90
1998–99	NY Rangers	70	9	53	62
TOTALS		1487	894	1963	2857

GM: Games

G: Goals

A: Assists

PTS: Points

GLOSSARY

assist player or players whose passes precede a goal; up to two assists may be credited for each goal

bodycheck to bump an opposing player with your hip or shoulder to block his progress or throw him off balance; legal only against a player who has the puck

blue lines painted lines running across the ice 60 feet in front of each goal; used to determine offsides

centering pass to pass the puck toward the middle of the ice to a teammate with a better angle at the goal

defensemen two players usually stationed in or near their defensive zone to help the goalie guard against attack

face-off dropping of the puck by the official between the sticks of two opposing players; starts play

free agent athlete who is free to play for any team he or she wishes, usually decided by the team willing to pay the most

hat trick for one player to score three goals in a single game

line ice hockey teams are made up of three-man forward lines and two-man defensive lines, who advance up the ice or defend their goal more or less side by side

offsides penalty that results from an attacking player having both skates on the goal side of the opposing team's blue line before the puck crosses the line; an offsides pass—sometimes called a two-line pass—occurs when an attacking player passes the puck from a point near his team's goal, across his own blue line and the red line

overtime additional period of play used to break a tie

penalty a violation of the rules for which a player must spend a certain number of minutes off the ice and his team must play one man down

period a hockey game is divided into three 20-minute periods of play

postseason period of time after the regular NHL season when the 16 teams with the best win-loss records have a playoff to determine who will win the Stanley Cup; there are four rounds of playoffs: the first eliminates eight teams, the next eliminates four, the next two, and the last two teams play for the championship

power play attack by a team at full strength against a team playing shorthanded due to a penalty

puck rubber disc, 1 inch thick and 3 inches in diameter

rebound puck that bounces off the goalie's body or equipment into position to be shot on goal again

red line painted line running across the center of the ice, dividing the rink in half

save act of a goalie in blocking a shot

slap shot the fastest form of shot, in which the shooter takes a high backswing and strikes the puck as hard as he can; slap shots have been measured at faster than 120 mph

stickhandling to move and control the puck with the stick

wrist shot a shot in which, without taking a backswing, the shooter snaps his wrists to shoot the puck; not as fast but more accurate than a slap shot

INDEX

Page numbers in *italics* indicate illustrations.

A
The Alan Thicke Show 41
Ali, Muhammad 90
Anderson, Glen 44
Angelou, Maya 90
Art Ross memorial trophies 26
Avco Cup 21

B
Badali, Gus 14
Bird, Larry 24
Boston Bruins 36, 58
Brantford Examiner 12, 13
Buchberger, Kelly 77

C
Calder Trophy 23
Calgary Flames 40, 45, 52, 58, 64, 66, 70
Canada Cup 27–29, 46–47, 55, 56, 67
Canadian National Institute for the Blind 36
Candy, John 63
Charles (Prince of Wales) 55–56
Chicago Blackhawks 40, 50, 83
Coffey, Paul 2, 44
Corson, Shayne 77

D
Daniels, Charlie 41
Davidson, John 85
Detroit Red Wings 54, 58, 79
Diana (Princess of Wales) 56

Dionne, Marcel 23, 29
Dole, Robert J. 90–91

E
Edmonton Oilers 18–24, 26, 27, 30–35, 37–39, 44, 47–48, 57–59, 64, 66
  Stanley Cup 44–46, 50–55, 59
  Wayne as captain 39–42
Esposito, Phil 25
Esso Medals of Achievement Program 92

F
Finland 28, 35
Foreman, George 91
Fox, Michael J. 63
Fuhr, Grant 52

G
Gilmour, Doug 78
Graham, Reverend Billy 91
Gretzky, Brent (brother) 45
Gretzky, Emma (daughter) 89
Gretzky, Glen (brother) 4
Gretzky, Janet (Jones) 55–56, *60,* 61
  engagement 57
  injury 83–84
  social life 63
  wedding 59–60
Gretzky, Keith (brother) 4
Gretzky, Kim (sister) 4
Gretzky, Mary (grandmother) 5–6
Gretzky, Paulina (daughter) 63
Gretzky, Phyllis (mother) 4, 5–6
Gretzky, Trevor (son) 73
Gretzky, Tristan (son) 88

Gretzky, Ty (son) 69
Gretzky, Walter (father) 4, 5–6, 7, 14, 23, 76
  illness 68–69
Gretzky, Wayne Douglas 3, 7, 17, 20, 22, 33, 38, 42, 49, 54, 60, 62, 65, 71, 78, 82, 93
  benched 19–20
  Canada Cup tournament 28
  captain of Oilers 39–42
  charity work 36, 91–92
  childhood 4–13
  final game 86
  information on 114–116
  injuries 44, 57, 69–70
  "Le Grand Gretzky" 12
  major leagues 16–31
  marriage 57
  Ninety-Nine All-Stars tour 75
  1,000 points 47
  playing style 30–31
  post-retirement 88–83
  record breaking 64–67
  signing with New York Rangers 80
  social life 63
  Stanley Cup 46
  traded to Los Angeles Kings 60
  traded to Oilers 18
  traded to St. Louis Blues 77–78
  TV commercials 36, 90
  typical day 48–50
  wedding 59–60
  WHA All-Star Game 20–22
Gualazzi, Brian 14

H
Hachborn, Lenny 11
Hanlon, Glen 22
Hawerchuck, Dale 54
Hockey Hall of Fame 87–88
hockey, information on 114–116
Howe, Gordie 10, 11, 20, 57, 65, 73
  record 1, 64–67
Howe, Marty 20
Huddy, Charlie 44

I
Indianapolis Racers 16–18
International Horatio Alger Award 90

K
Keenan, Mike 77
Kerr, Alan 65
Kurri, Jari 44, 54

L
Lady Byng Trophy 23
Lafleur, Guy 26, 29, 47
Lemieux, Mario 51, 56, 57
Los Angeles Kings 23, 33–34, 47, 50, 53, 61–77
  bankruptcy 76–77
  Stanley Cup finals 72–73
Lowe, Kevin 22

M
MacPherson, Murray "Muzz" 15
Mahovlich, Frank 6
McLean, Kirk 73
McNall, Bruce 76, 77
Melrose, Barry 69
Messier, Mark 22, 44, 54, 58, 80–81
Montreal Canadiens 26, 72–73
Morrison, Scott 88
Moss, Joey 18
Moss, Vicky 18, 55

N
Nadrofsky Steelers 8, 9, 11
Nagano, Japan, 1998 Summer Olympics 84
National Basketball Association (NBA) 104
National Hockey League (NHL) 9, 13, 16, 24–25, 37
  All-Stars 57, 75, 85
  financial agreement with WHA 21–22
  Hall of Fame 47
  labor problems 73–75
  Most Valuable Player Award 85
  NHL Player of the Year 26
  Rookie of the Year Award 23
  scouts 15
New Jersey Devils 44
New York Islanders 27, 37, 41, 42, 45, 65
New York Rangers 80–93
New York Times Magazine 50–51
NHL Official Guide and Record Book 1

Ninety-Nine All-Stars tour *75*
Norris Division 26

O
Olympics 27, 84, 90
Ontario Hockey Association 13
Ontario Minor Hockey Association 8
Order of Canada Medal 84–85
Orr, Bobby 11, 25

P
Perreault, Gil 29
Philadelphia Flyers 23, 50, 54, 82
Phoenix Coyotes 89
Pittsburgh Penguins 86
Pocklington, Peter 35, 60, 61, 76
Podnieks, Andrew 24
Powell, Colin 91
professional athletes
  advancement, career 105–107
  books on 111–112
  earnings 107–108
  educational requirements 100–102
  employers of 104
  employment outlook 110
  exploring field 102–104
  how to become 97–110
  job description 97–100
  organizations 112–113
  requirements 100–102
  sports agents 105
  starting out 104–105
  work environment 108–110

Q
Quebec Nordiques 39

R
Rea, John 13
Recchi, Mark 85
Rendezvous '87 53
Richler, Mordecai 50–51
Ronald McDonald House 91–92
Rookie of the Year Award 23
Russia 67–68

S
Salt Lake City Winter Olympics (2002) 90
Sather, Glen 19, 32, 37, 39, 81
Sault Ste. Marie Greyhounds 14–15
Sinden, Harry 36
Smith, Billy 41
Soviet Union 29, 35, 47, 56
  Cold War 67–68
  Moscow Summer Olympics (1980) 27
Stanley Cup 32, 38, 41, 43–60, 70, 72–73
Stastny, Peter 39, 47
St. Louis Blues 77–78
Sweden 29

T
Team Canada 34–35, 46, 56, 81, 84, 89–90
Team North America 85
time line 94–96
Toronto Maple Leafs 6, 71, 79
Toronto Toros 13
Torrey, Bill 37

U
U.S. Department of Labor 107

V
Vancouver Canucks 71
Vernon, Mike 58

W
Wally Bauer Trophy 8
Wally's Coliseum 8
Warhol, Andy 42
Wayne Gretzky Fantasy Camp 91
Winfrey, Oprah 91
Winnipeg Jets 45, 53–54
Woods, Tiger 90
World Cup 81
World Hockey Association (WHA) 13, 16
  All-Star Game 20–22
  financial agreement with NHL 21–22
World Hockey Championships 34–35
World Junior Championship 15

ABOUT THE AUTHOR

Michael Benson has written young-adult biographies of Lance Armstrong, Ronald Reagan, Bill Clinton, William Howard Taft, Malcolm X, Muhammad Ali, Dale Earnhardt, and Gloria Estefan. He is the former editor of *All-Time Baseball Greats, Fight Game,* and *Stock Car Spectacular* magazines. He is the author of 30 books, including *The Encyclopedia of the JFK Assassination* and *Complete Idiot's Guides to NASA, the CIA, National Security, Aircraft Carriers, Submarines,* and *Modern China.* Originally from Rochester, New York, he is a graduate of Hofstra University. He enjoys his life with his wife and two children in Brooklyn, New York, and his goal is to one day write the Great American Novel.